Mel Bay's Modern VIOLA METHOD GRADE 1

www.melbay.com/21547BCDEB

by Martin Norgaard & Laurie Scott

Audio Contents

Visit us on the Web at www.melbay.com — E-mail us at email@melbay.com

Foreword

Two schools of thought exist concerning beginning string instruction. One school believes that the technical foundation should precede the introduction of music notation. The other school of thought believes that music reading and technique can be taught concurrently from the beginning. Good teachers can embrace either approach, sequence lessons logically, and end up with a well-rounded student. The danger however is that the deemphasized element in either approach can leave the student lacking reading ability, correct initial posture, or tied to a page of music because aural skills have not been developed.

For the very young beginning student that has not yet encountered language reading, teaching music by rote seems the logical choice. However, for the school-aged and adult beginner, the choice becomes less clear. The solution seems to suggest a method that emphasizes the development of consistent correct technique, while developing aural and music literacy skills simultaneously. These goals are the foundation of this method.

This method and music reading provides a fundamental challenge: The easiest music symbol to read (the whole note) is one of the most difficult to play, because it requires the student to use the entire bow. Current well-founded methodology starts beginning players with short stopped bow strokes at the middle of the bow. This book introduces various rhythms that require short bow strokes without explaining the logic behind the notation. Instead, the rhythms are presented with phonological equivalents that provide the rhythmic translation. This, in combination with the companion audio, helps resolve the juxtaposition of rhythm reading and the sequence of technical development.

Many different types of performers use the viola in a wide variety of musical venues. Whether classical, jazz, rock or fiddle, successful violists performing any style of music share common standards related to excellence of intonation, bow technique, tone and musicianship. This book seeks to develop these skills concurrently, building each lesson around a specific technical issue while combining music literacy, ear training, and performance concepts.

This book can be utilized in a variety of teaching and learning situations. As a stand-alone text, the book can serve to introduce adults and school-aged beginners to the instrument and provide instruction related to the fundamental skills necessary to play the viola in a technically correct and musically satisfying way. The book can also serve as a partner book for students in school string programs by providing a review of initial skills, an introduction to advanced technique, ear training exercises and an anthology of repertoire. The teaching points of the chosen literature can also supplement Suzuki Viola repertoire and provide students and parents involved in Suzuki lessons with additional ear training activities, and music literacy exercises.

The tunes in this volume are varied stylistically and include folk tunes from various cultures and original and classic melodies chosen for their musical value and accessibility. The goal of this book is to facilitate the development of skill while providing opportunities to think and hear musically.

Martin Norgaard and Laurie Scott, November, 2007

Acknowledgements

We would like to thank the following people for their contribution to this book:

Proofreading – Melissa Becker, William Dick, Jessica Embach, Andrew Strietelmeier.

Photos – Andrew Noble, Daniela Pennycook, Estevan Uriegas, Brennan Wong.

Orchestral Accompaniment – The University of Texas String Project Faculty.

Table of Contents

Buying or Renting?

Deciding whether or not to buy or rent an instrument is a big decision. If you already own a viola, be sure it is adjusted properly. A bridge that is too high, frayed strings, uneven fingerboards, cracks or open seams, are just a few of the problems that can come with instruments that have been out of use for an extended period of time. If you are purchasing an instrument, it is well worth the money to buy from a reputable instrument dealer who will be sure you leave the store with an instrument and bow that are the correct size, and in good playing condition.

As with buying, when renting an instrument, take the time to be sure the instrument and bow are in good condition and properly adjusted. Get to know the instrument dealers in your area and find someone you can trust to help you make these important decisions. Depending on the rental fees, it may very well be worth it to purchase the instrument at the outset. Many stores have rent-to-own contracts that can help you finance your purchase. Whether you rent or buy, the quality of the viola will affect your rate of progress, your concept of tone, and your overall enjoyment while learning to play the instrument.

If you decide to buy an instrument, you will be faced with the decision of buying an old viola or a new viola. Many people automatically think that an old instrument is better than a new instrument. This is absolutely not the case. Old violas may look charming but sound terrible. Repair or restoration of an old instrument may also be substantial. The best thing to do is to try a variety of instruments, or better yet, have someone play the instruments for you. Listen for a loud open sound. Be wary of muffled or nasal sounding instruments and don't let anyone talk you into buying something that will "break in" and sound better over time. You may listen to twenty violas and like the one that is the least expensive. Choose a comfortable price range and try a wide variety of instruments. Violas not only sound different but also feel different to play. The height and shape of the bridge and width of the neck can be quite different on every instrument. Choose a viola that feels comfortable to play.

You may be fortunate enough to have a reputable dealer in your town. If this is the case, you will have the luxury of spending time in a shop, listening to violas at your leisure. If not, there are many dealers that will mail violas anywhere in the world. You can try two or three at a time, but be prepared to pay for shipping and insurance on instruments that get mailed back to the dealer.

You may buy a viola that already has a bow in the case. If not, you will also need to choose a bow. Bows, like violas, come in all different price ranges. Bows can be made from wood, fiberglass or carbonfiber. No matter what the stick of the bow is made from, you should always have horsehair on the bow, not fiberglass. When choosing a bow, be sure that the stick of the bow is strong and not warped. The bow stick should be straight and strong, but also have enough spring in it to "bounce" on the string. Use a viola bow NOT a violin bow on your instrument. Viola bows are heavier and have slightly different dimensions than a violin bow.

It is best to have someone with experience help you choose your instrument and bow if possible.

Before you start playing, you need to put on a shoulder rest, rosin the bow, and tune the instrument. These topics are covered in detail on pages 82–87.

The Viola & Bow

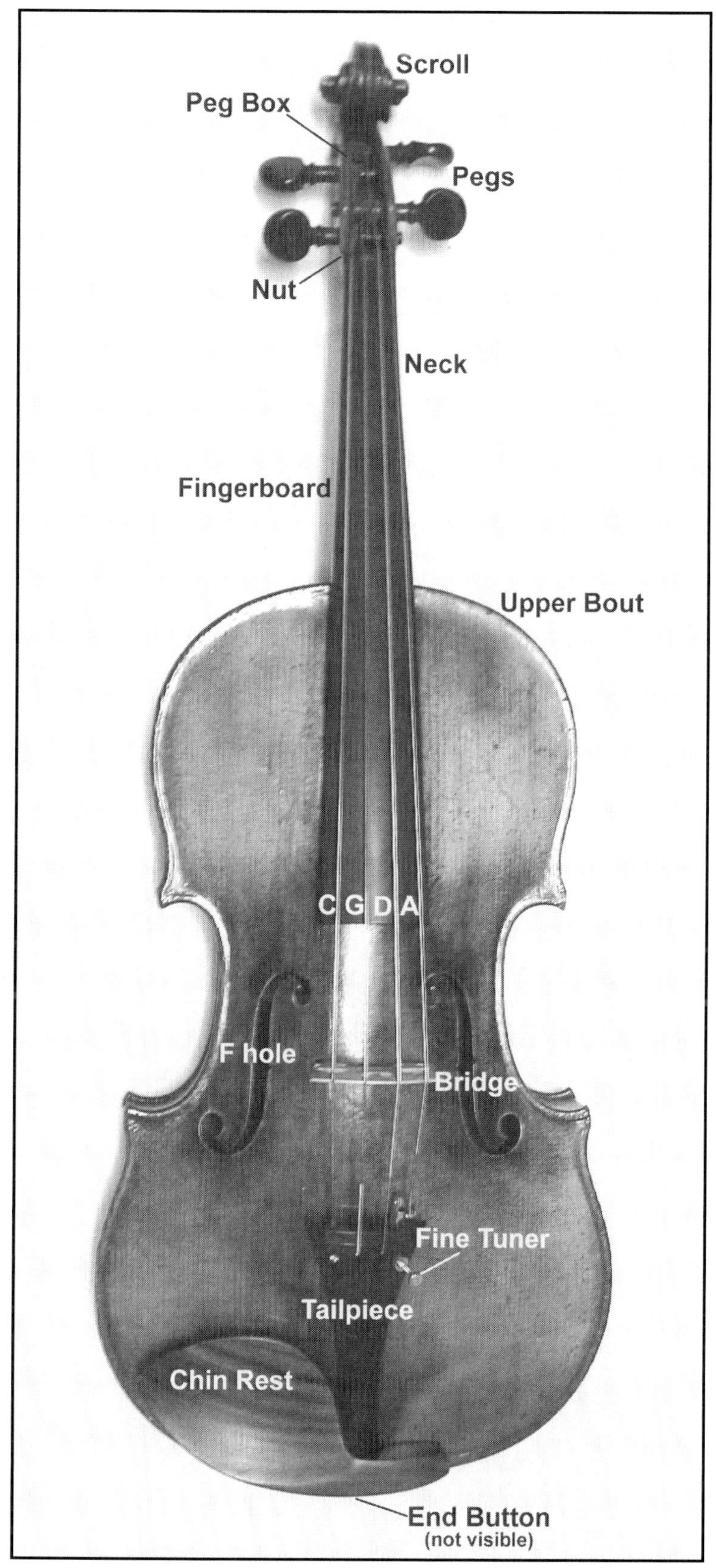

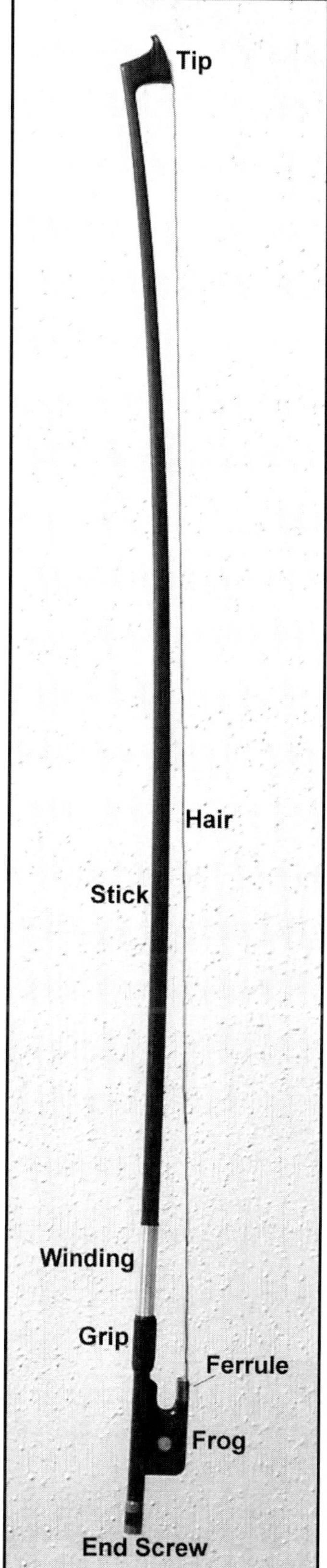

Lesson 1
Holding and Plucking the Viola

What You Will Learn:

Technique: To hold the viola in rest position and playing position, and to play pizzicato
Music Literacy: The names of the open strings
Ear Training: To recognize the open strings by ear
Tunes: It's the Pizz & Plucking the Blues

Technique:

Goal: To hold the viola in rest position

What To Do:

1) Stand with your feet slightly apart.

2) Cradle the viola under the right arm with the back of the instrument resting against your side, right hand supporting the upper bout of the instrument and the scroll pointing straight ahead and slightly up. Be careful not to let the right arm press too hard on the bridge or tailpiece. This is called "rest position."

3) Hang your bow on your right index finger.

This Is Why:
Establishing a relaxed position before actually setting the viola on the shoulder can help keep you from transferring unnecessary tension into the fundamental posture setup. Initially, the viola should be placed while you are in standing position so total body balance can be achieved. From a relaxed standing rest position, you can now practice setting the instrument on the shoulder in playing position. When taking breaks from playing or practicing, return the instrument to rest position.

Goal: To hold the viola in playing position

Put down the bow. We will use the bow in Lesson 4.

What To Do:

1) From rest position, put your left hand on the upper bout of the viola with fingers on the front and thumb on the back so you have a firm hold.

2) Release the instrument from under your arm and hold it straight out to your left.

3) Turn the instrument over, so the scroll is pointing towards the floor and the tailpiece towards the ceiling.

4) Point the endpin towards your neck and turn your head towards the left.

5) Slowly bring the instrument toward your neck and place the viola on your shoulder. Turn your head to the left and place your jaw in the chin rest. Make sure your jaw bone "hooks" over the edge of the chin rest. Now take your left hand and cross it over to rest on your right shoulder. This will help bring the shoulder under the viola for support.

This Is Why:

You may ask yourself, "Why can't I just put the viola under my chin and start playing?" Feeling comfortable while playing the viola should certainly be one of your first goals. You should be able to consistently place the instrument in a comfortable position that allows total freedom of the left arm, with both shoulders, head, and neck muscles relaxed. By going through a series of steps, correct placement of the viola will become natural and routine. Once the instrument is in playing position, imagine yourself engaged in a conversation. If the viola were invisible, would your head and neck look like they were in a natural position? If not, you probably tilted your head in one direction or another. This tilting can cause tension and eventually keep you from being able to perform advanced techniques.

Goal: Pizzicato

Definition:
Pizzicato – Pizzicato is the musical term for "plucking" that is derived from the Italian word for "pinched." We will use pizzicato to play our first tune.

What To Do:

1) Go from rest position to playing position.
2) Move the left hand to the upper bout of the viola.
3) Make a "thumbs up" with the right thumb.
4) Place the thumb against the right side of the fingerboard about 1 inch from the end of the fingerboard.
5) Pluck the strings with your index finger without moving the thumb. Be sure to pluck the strings over the fingerboard, not between the fingerboard and bridge. You will get a much better sound and avoid the "rosin" zone.

This Is Why:
By resting the thumb on the side of the fingerboard, we create resistance for our pizzicato finger and more stability for the instrument. By plucking over the fingerboard, you not only avoid getting your finger covered with rosin, but also achieve a resonant tone.

Music Literacy:
Goal: Learning the Musical Alphabet

Definition:
Note names – The musical alphabet is derived from the letter names. Notes are named using the letters A, B, C, D, E, F and G.

The viola strings are tuned to the notes: C, G, D and A. Because these notes are five letter names away from each other, we say the viola is tuned in fifths. C is the lowest pitched string and therefore the thickest; A is the highest pitched and thinnest string.

What To Do:
Recite a repeating musical alphabet remembering to only use letters A-G, NOT A-Z!!

Ear Training:
Goal: To recognize the open strings by ear

Tr. 5

What To Do:
Listen to the notes being playing on the CD. You will hear each note four times. Pluck the string that matches the note you hear four times.

Tr. 6

It's the Pizz

A A A A
D D D D
G G G G
C C C C
G G G G
D D D D
A A A A

What To Do:
Read the names of the open strings and pluck along. Notice that the note names are placed so they are easy to read. Play along with the CD.

When you read music, move your feet to allow your entire body to turn so the scroll is pointing toward the music stand. This MUSIC READING POSITION will allow you to see your left hand AND the music without changing your playing position.

Tr. 7

Plucking the Blues

D D D D G G G G D D D D D D D D

G G G G G G G G D D D D G G G G

A A A A G G G G D D D D D D D D

What To Do:
Read and play along like you did in "It's the Pizz." This piece is a bit harder to read because the names of the open strings are placed on the same line. After you get to the end of the first line jump to the next line and read from the beginning just like you do when you read words.

Lesson 2
Using the Right Hand and Note Duration

What You Will Learn:

Technique:	To make a the bow hold shape
	To use the bow hold shape for balance
Music Literacy:	The value and length of whole, half and quarter notes
Ear Training:	To recognize note duration by ear
	To imitate rhythm and pitch
Tunes:	Stop, Look and Listen! & A Skip and a Jump

Technique:

Goal: Making a bow hold shape

What To Do:

With your right hand, make a circle using your two middle fingers and thumb. Place the pads of the middle fingers on the thumb nail to make a "bow bunny" shape.

This Is Why:

The "bow bunny" shape lets you make the shape of a real bow hold without having to worry about supporting the weight of the entire bow.

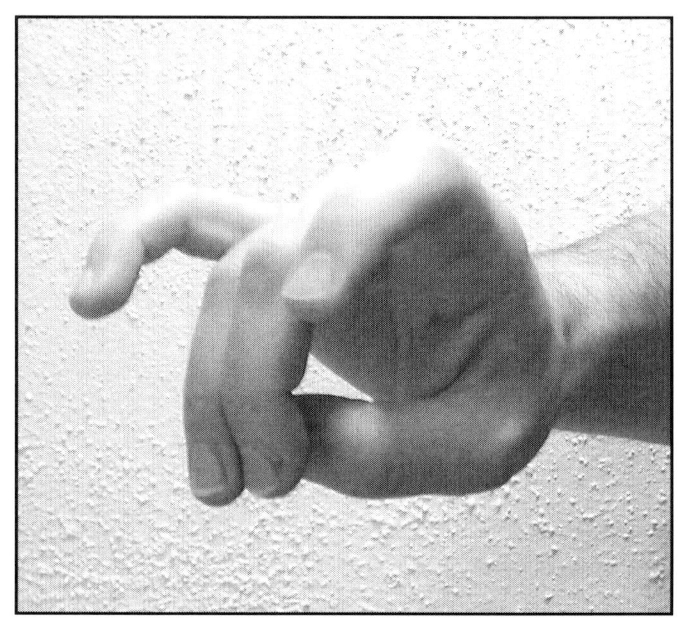

Goal: Using the Bow Hold Shape for Balance

What To Do:

1) Hold the end of a pencil with your left hand.
2) Make the "bow bunny" shape with the right hand and let the "bow bunny" "bite" the pencil. You will now be holding the pencil between your middle fingers and your thumb.
3) Let the "ears" of the bunny (your index finger and pinky) fall on to the top of the pencil. The tip of the pinky sits on top of the pencil and the index finger touches the pencil lightly in the crease closest to the nail. Check your hand to see that all the joints of your fingers are curved.

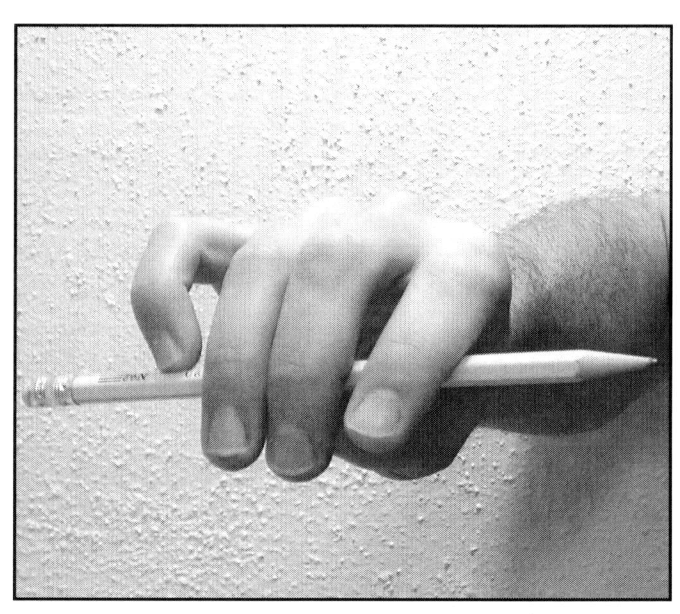

4) Push the bunny's "ears" up and down to make a seesaw motion. Feel the bow pivot on the tip of your thumb. Make sure the thumb is still bent.

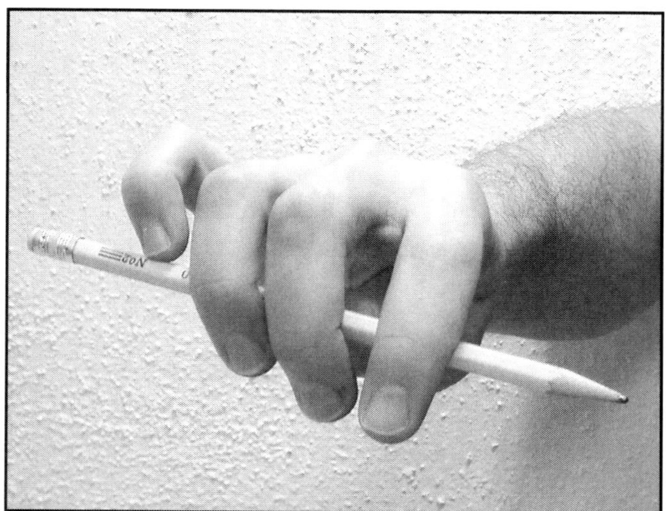

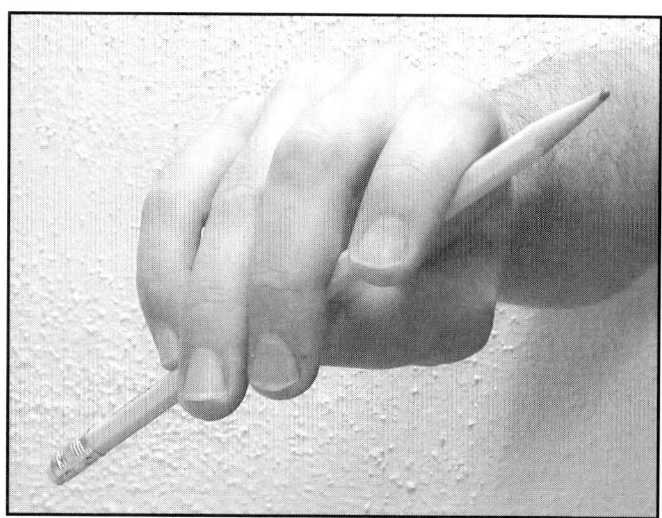

This Is Why:
Using the "bow bunny" shape lets you feel the way your fingers will balance and control the real bow. It is important to establish a comfortable and functional bow hold right from the beginning so that you can play beginning AND advanced bow strokes. The seesaw motion develops finger flexibility and previews the various hand shapes you will need later. Keeping all the joints of your bow hand curved will make it possible to play very smooth bow changes.

Music Literacy:
Goal: Learning the value and length of whole, half and quarter notes.

Definition:
Notes - Each symbol that we call a note gives us information related to pitch and duration. In other words, the notes tell us what things will sound like AND how long the sound will last.

Pulse - Each piece of music has its own "heartbeat" or pulse. When you tap your foot while listening to music you are probably tapping to the pulse. You can count along with the pulse.

Beat – Whatever type of note that corresponds with the pulse "gets the beat." When we count the number of beats we therefore count a particular type of note. We could count any value of note, but most often we count quarter notes or eighth notes.

Rhythm of notes - The rhythm of notated music is decoded by assigning a certain number of beats to each type of note.

The mathematics of music – The value of notes refer to their relative relationship. A whole note is the same length as two half notes which is the same as four quarters etc. In math it would look like this:

$$1 = 1/2 + 1/2 = 1/4 + 1/4 + 1/4 + 1/4 = 1/8 + 1/8 + 1/8 + \dots\dots\dots \text{ etc.}$$

This is what a whole note, half note and quarter note look like:

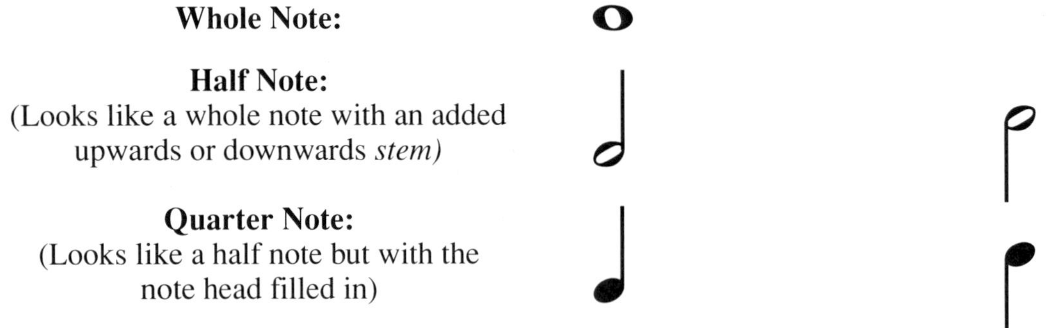

What To Do:
In the space to the right of the notes above, draw exact copies of each type of note.

Definition:
Bar or Measure - A small grouping of beats. The lines between the groupings are called *barlines*.

4/4 Time signature (written as C) - Very often western music is written in measures that consist of values equivalent to one whole note. We will use this type of measure exclusively until Lesson 14. Remember, a whole note equals two half notes or four quarter notes. If the pulse corresponds to the quarter notes, then we would count four beats in each measure. It then follows that half notes receive two counts and whole notes, four counts.

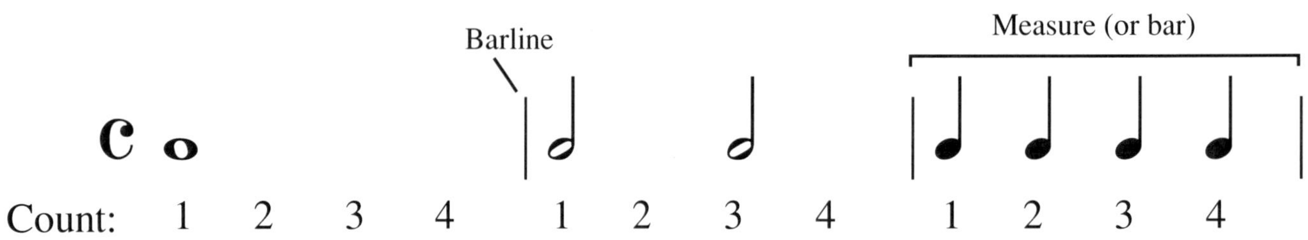

Ear Training:
Goal: To recognize note duration by ear

 Tr. 8

What To Do:

1) Write the numbers 1-10 below each other on a piece of paper. You will listen to ten notes on track 8 from the CD. As you figure out what each note is, write the correct note value next to the number.

2) Listen to the clicks and notes on the CD. The clicks will tell you the duration of each note. You can also count along.

3) After each note is played, write down which type of note you think it is. Remember whole notes get four clicks or beats, half notes get two, and quarter notes get one.

4) You can check your answers by looking at the answer key on page 81.

Tr. 9

Stop, Look, and Listen!

M. Norgaard & L. Scott

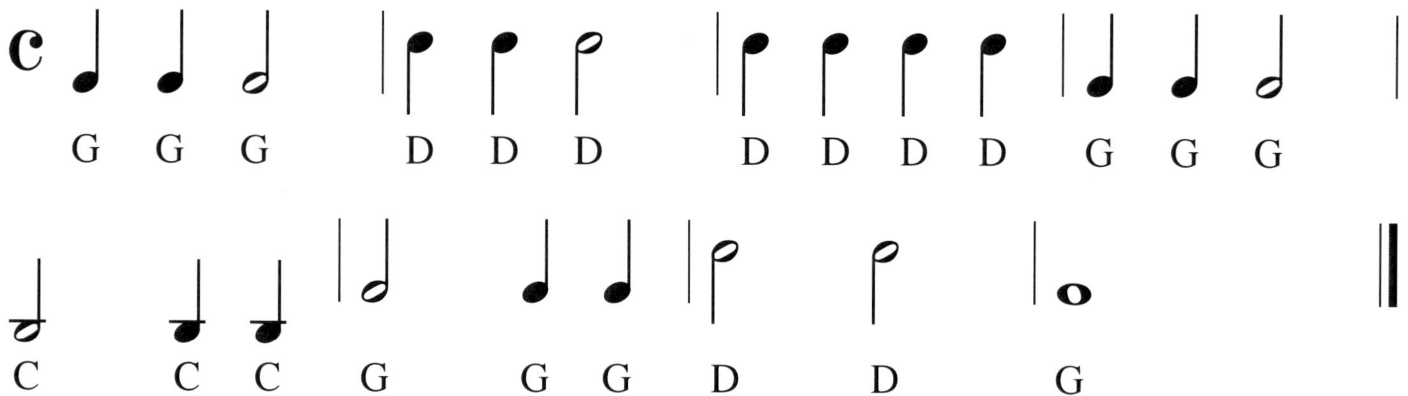

What To Do:

1) Listen to the CD. You may be able to learn the song by just listening to the CD.
2) Next, listen to the CD while you look at the notation above WITHOUT plucking. Do you recognize the notes as written above?
3) Pluck the tune above without the CD. Remember, if you look at the book while playing, the book should be on a music stand so you can maintain a good playing posture.
4) Now try to pluck along with the CD.
5) You may have noticed the note C has a line crossing the stem. You will learn more about this line in Lesson 5.
6) Also note that the last barline is a double line. A double barline indicates the end of a song.

Tr. 10

A Skip and a Jump

M. Norgaard

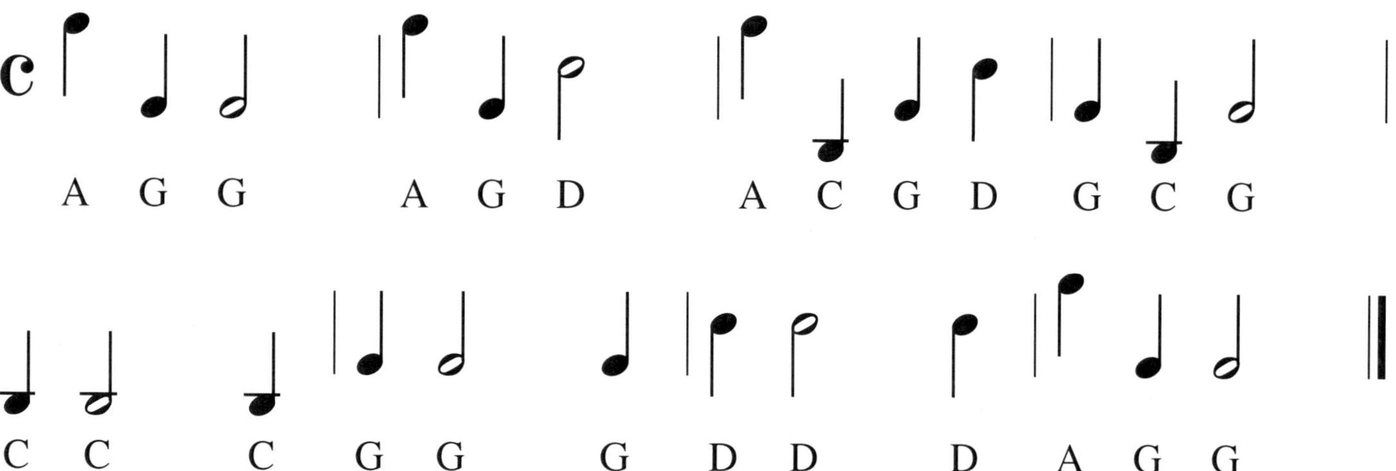

What To Do:

Follow the same steps as in "Stop, Look, and Listen!" This tune is a bit more difficult because it jumps around.

Lesson 3
Left Hand Posture

<u>What You Will Learn:</u>

Technique: To set the fingers of the left hand on the string
Music Literacy: The names of the notes on the D string
Ear Training: To identify notes going up (ascending) or going down (descending)
Tunes: Au Claire De La Lune & Ode To Joy

<u>Technique:</u>

Goal: Setting the fingers of the left hand

What To Do:

1) While seated, hold your viola in guitar position.

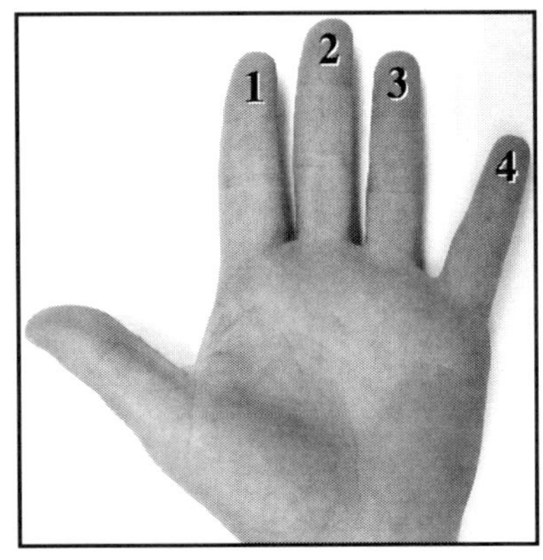

2) Line up the crease at the base of the index finger (*first finger*) of your left hand on the neck where the black and white wood meet, a little behind the first finger tape.

3) Gently let the thumb rest on the neck. Keep the thumb across from the first finger and make sure it doesn't bend.

4) Bend your first finger and place the tip directly on the first finger tape. Stand the finger tall creating a little "table top" between the first and second joint.

5) Now set the middle finger (*second finger*) on the second finger tape, and so on, until all four fingers are set on the D string. Look at your left hand to be sure all the joints in each finger are curved.

6) Keeping your fingers on the fingerboard, use your right hand to place the viola in playing position.

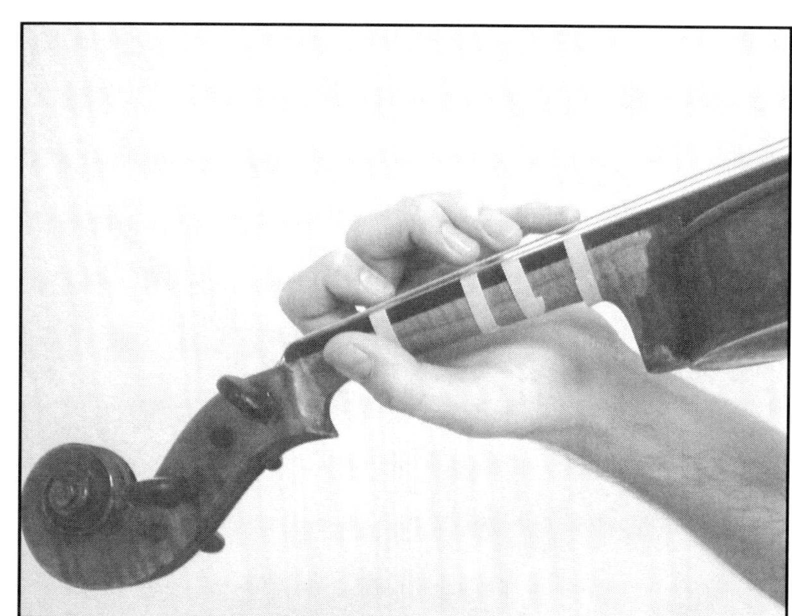

7) Your left wrist should be straight, fingers tall, and all joints curved. Never let the palm of your hand touch the neck of the viola.

8) With the viola in playing position, gently lift the fingers off the fingerboard but KEEP THEM HOVERING OVER THE FINGER TAPES. You will now only have two points of contact with the neck of the viola: the thumb, and the base of the first finger.

9) While supporting the viola with your head and shoulder, drop your left hand to your side, then reset the left-hand fingers on the fingerboard as pictured.

10) Practice resetting your left hand, but this time from standing playing position.

Goal: Playing all the fingers on the D string pizzicato

1) Set your left hand as described above.

2) Get the right hand into pizzicato position.

3) Pizzicato using fingers in ascending order on the D string: open D, 1, 2, 3, 4. Check to be sure you have maintained curved joints in every finger. Notice when you put fingers on the string the pitch gets higher (ascends).

4) Pizzicato using fingers in descending order: 4, 3, 2, 1, open D. Notice when you take fingers off the string the pitch gets lower (descends).

This Is Why:

The posture of the left hand will initially affect your intonation and tone, however a faulty left hand posture will detrimentally affect all advanced technique. The ability to shift, vibrate, and play double stops is dependent on a relaxed left hand that consistently approaches the string the same way.

Music Literacy:
Goal: Learning the names of the notes on the D string

We learned in Lesson 1 that the musical alphabet goes from A to G. Sometimes the notes have "last names," like sharp (♯) or flat (♭). These last names tell us exactly where on the fingerboard to put our finger to get the pitch the note name indicates. Now we will learn the names of the notes on the D string. Since the open string is called D and we follow the alphabet, the next four notes are, E, F♯, G and A. F♯ is the only note we will play right now that has a last name. Look at the note names below and notice which finger plays which note. The fingerings are written with small numbers above the notes.

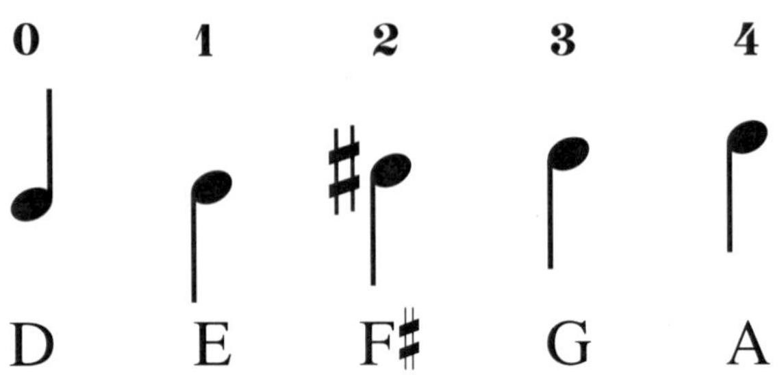

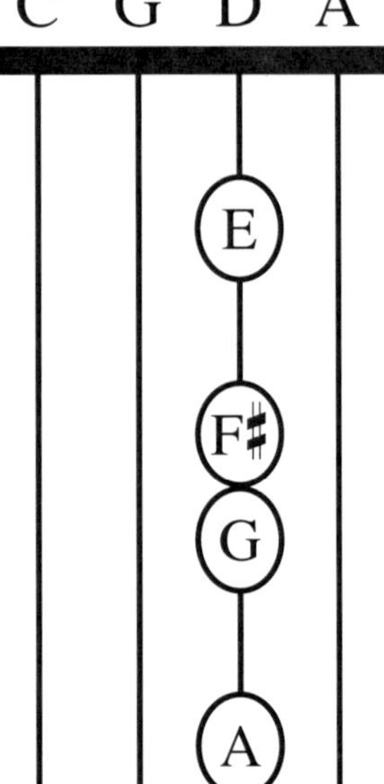

You should have tapes on your fingerboard that will help you find the place for each finger on the D string.

What To Do:
Repeat the exercise on the previous page using note names. Before you pluck each note say the note name. In others words:

1) Say "D".
2) Pluck the D string.
3) Say "E".
4) Pluck the D string while holding down the first finger.
5) Continue up to the 4th finger, A, and back down to D.

Ear Training:
Goal: To identify notes going up (ascending) or going down (descending)

Tr. 11

What To Do:
1) Listen to four different examples that go either from low to high (ascending) or high to low (descending).
2) In each example you will hear pitches in ascending or descending patterns. All the patterns will be played on the D string.
3) Identify the direction of the pattern as ascending or descending. You can write it down and check your answers on page 81.

Tr. 12

Au Claire De La Lune

French Folk Song

What To Do:

1) Listen to "Au Claire De La Lune" and without your viola, silently tap the fingering using your left-hand fingers against your thumb.

2) Put your viola in playing position, set left hand for fingering and set right hand in pizzicato position.

3) Imitate the rhythm and pitch you hear on the CD. You will use the notes on the D string in ascending and descending order. If you hear the notes ascend, put fingers down. If you hear the notes descend, take fingers away.

4) Although you do not yet know the names of the notes on the other strings, try the same melody on the other strings. If you think about it, you probably can figure out at least the "first names" of the pitches on the others strings using your "alphabet logic."

5) Compose your own song by using ascending and descending patterns on the D string.

Tr. 13

Ode to Joy

L. Beethoven

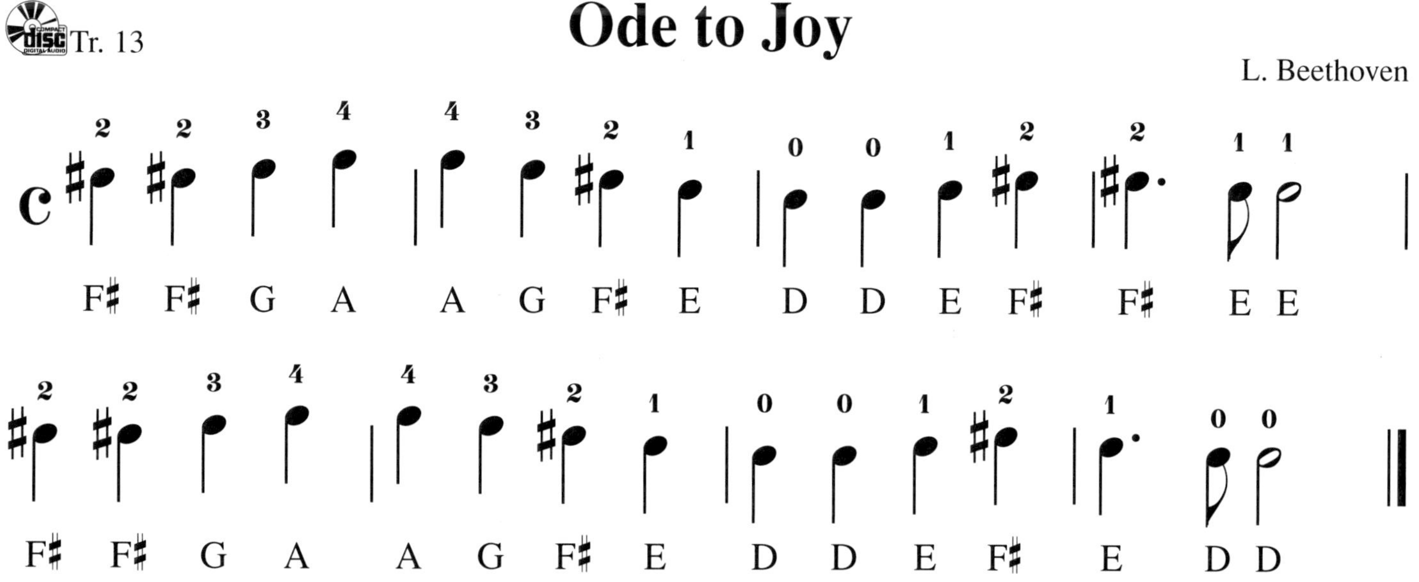

What To Do:

Follow the same steps as in "Au Claire De La Lune." This tune is a bit more difficult because it uses all four fingers. Set the second finger in the first measure without putting down the first finger.

Lesson 4
Setting the Bow

<u>What You Will Learn:</u>

Technique:	To make a professional bow hold
	To set the bow at the "square" of the arm
Music Literacy:	The definition of Alto clef and staff
Tune:	A String Concerto

<u>Technique:</u>
Goal: Making a professional bow hold

What To Do:

1) From a standing position, take hold of the bow in the middle of the stick with your left hand. Be careful not to touch the hair of the bow. Make the bow bunny shape with your right hand and let the bow bunny "bite" the bow stick near the middle of the bow.

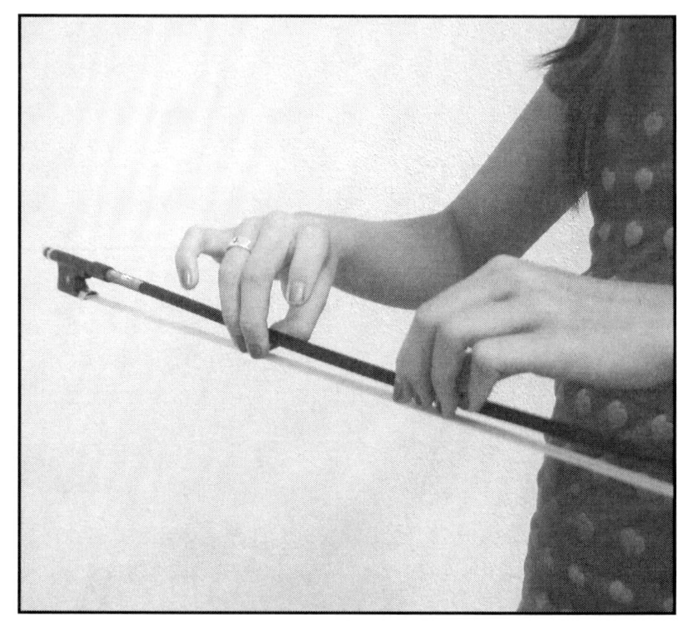

2) Slide the bow bunny toward the frog of the bow until the thumb "dead ends" against the edge of the frog. Your thumb touches the bow, half on the edge of the frog and half on the stick. It will feel like the stick of the bow is gently wedged between your thumbnail and the skin at the tip of the thumb. Your thumb will be bent and should stay bent. Your thumb will be near, but not necessarily touching, the hair of the bow. Make sure your thumb is not protruding through the frog.

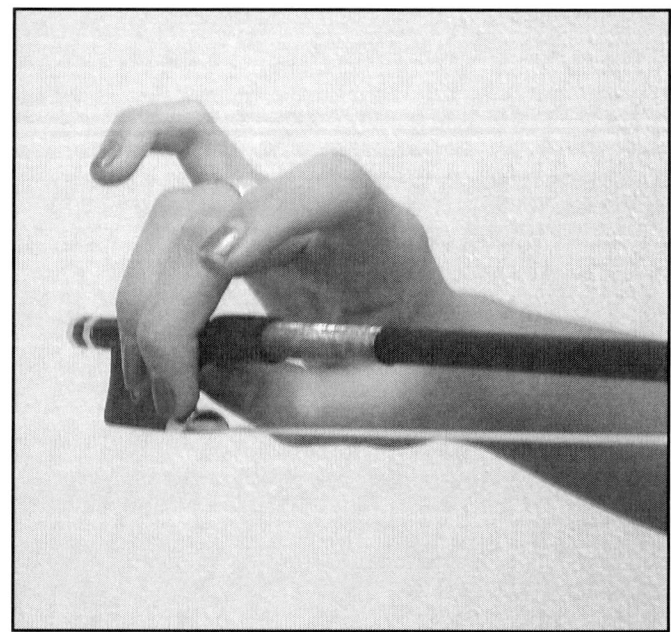

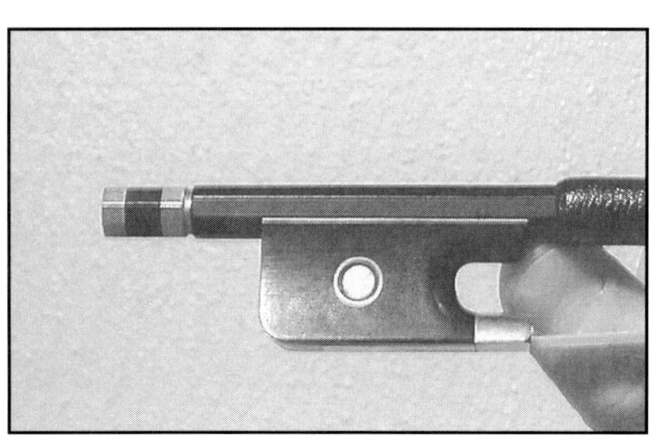

3) Let the ears of the "bunny" fall on the top of the bow stick. The fingers should be naturally spaced with the curved pinky sitting on top of the stick. The index finger will sit on the winding or grip of the bow near the joint closest to the nail.

4) Check to see that the middle and ring fingers are far enough over the stick so that the first crease is touching the wood. The middle finger should touch, or nearly touch, the ferrule.

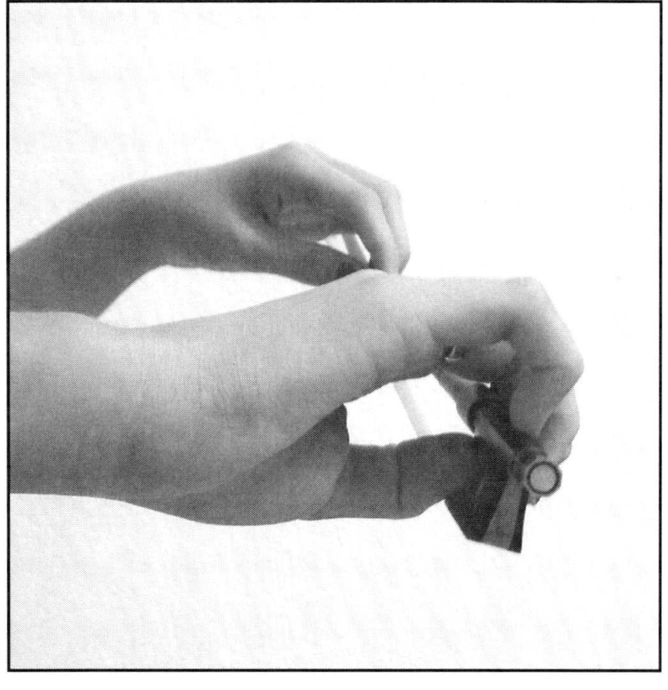

ALL JOINTS SHOULD BE CURVED!!

5) Let go of the bow with your left hand and turn the bow so the tip is pointed toward the ceiling.

6) Your hand should be relaxed and the joints of all the fingers should be curved.

7) Practice setting your bow hold many times, ending each time with the bow tip pointed at the ceiling.

This Is Why:
It is vital that the relationship of the fingers to the stick is consistent and correct from the very beginning stages of study. It is possible to hold the bow "any old way" and still be able to make a sound, but that's not the point. The shape, not strength, of the bow hand controls the balance of the bow, the point of contact, and the tone.

The reason we tip the bow toward the ceiling after the bow hand is set, is to take the responsibility of balancing the bow away from the pinky. The pinky is the weakest finger and until it has been strengthened and has become accustomed to balancing the bow, it should not be taxed.

To accommodate ALL styles of bowing including all advanced bow strokes, the joints of the fingers need to act like "shock absorbers", hence the curved joints. Playing with stiff joints and straight fingers makes anything that has to do with smooth bowing or bouncing strokes very difficult to achieve.

Goal: Setting the bow at the "square of the arm"

What To Do:

1) Place the viola in playing position.

2) With your right hand relaxed and in a bow bunny shape, place fingers in the bow hold position on the frog of the bow. Be sure all joints are curved.

3) Turn the bow so the tip is toward the ceiling.

4) Slowly bring the bow toward the viola and set the bow on the A string halfway between the bridge and the fingerboard with your right arm positioned at a 90 degree angle. A "square" shape will be created by your arm, your body, and the viola. You have now set the bow at what is called the *square of the arm*. Your right arm should be relaxed, hanging comfortably and naturally at your side. The place where the bow meets the string is called the *contact point*. You should strive to keep the contact point of the bow midway between the bridge and the fingerboard.

5) Take the bow away from the instrument and practice resetting the bow on the A string at the square of the arm many times. Try to land on the string without making any sound.

6) Say "Mississippi Stop Stop". Now move your bow down and up using short strokes matching each syllable of "Mis-sis-sip-pi Stop Stop". Move your bow down towards the floor on the first syllable "Mis" then back up on "sis" and so on. Only move the bow about 2 inches on each bow stroke. The only joint you use to do this stroke is the elbow. The elbow works like a hinge.

YOU JUST PLAYED YOUR FIRST BOWED NOTES!!!

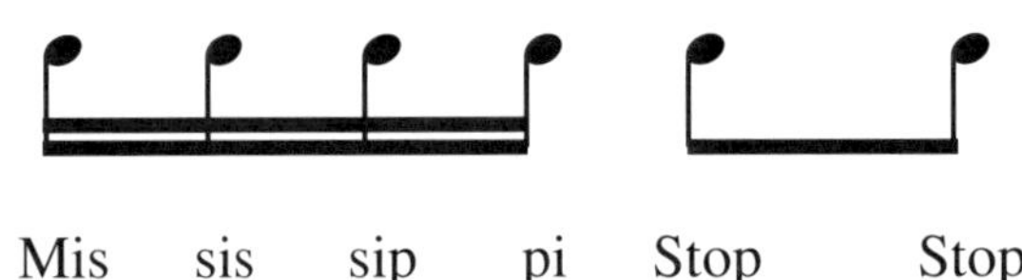

Mis sis sip pi Stop Stop

This is how the "Mississippi Stop Stop" rhythm looks in notation. It uses sixteenth notes and eighth notes. We will discuss these note values in Lesson 24. The important thing for you to do now is to recognize the rhythm the words make when notated. At the end of this lesson we will learn a tune that consists exclusively of this rhythm.

This Is Why:

The square of the arm is a great starting place to begin practicing with the viola and bow together. By using only the middle section of the bow, you should be able to practice maintaining the professional bow hold shape. Limiting the amount of bow you use will allow you to experience the three most important elements of tone: weight, speed, and contact point, without losing the shape of your bow hand by traveling to the extremes of the bow.

Music Literacy:
Goal: Clef sign and musical staff defined

Definitions:
Music staff - The music staff is a set of five lines and four spaces from which we identify pitch symbols.

C Clef or Alto Clef - Violists read music in what is known as alto clef. Alto clef is distinguished by the use of a clef sign called the "C" clef. While violists primarily use the alto clef, the treble clef (or G clef) is used when viola music is written in high registers. Because alto clef is most notably reserved for violists, it is sometimes called "viola clef." The word clef is derived from the Latin word "clavis" or key. The clef is a sign that defines a line on the staff, to which all other lines and spaces of the staff are related.

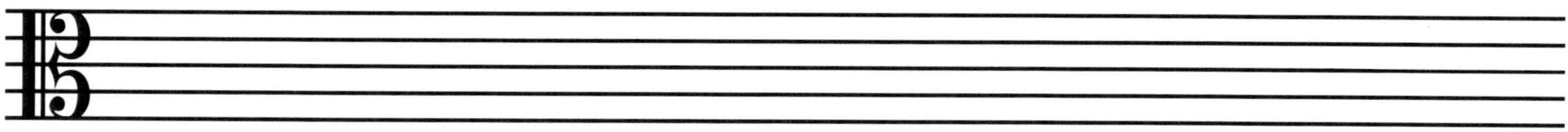

What To Do:
Copy the alto clef shape several times on the staff above.

Tr. 14

A String Concerto

M. Norgaard

What To Do:

1) Set your viola in playing position and set your bow on the A string at the square of the arm.

2) Play the Mississippi Stop Stop rhythm seven times then take a little break. No need to follow the notation above. Just listen to the CD. Notice the violist on the CD alters the tempo slightly at the end of each line.

3) The symbol ⊓ over the first note means you move your bow down toward the floor (*down bow*).

Lesson 5
The Seesaw and Bowing First Finger

<u>**What You Will Learn:**</u>

Technique:	To find the balance point on the bow and the Seesaw exercise
	To use the left hand first finger and bow at the same time
Music Literacy:	Placing open string notes on the staff
Ear Training:	To use singing to help you learn pieces
Tune:	Who's on First?

<u>**Technique:**</u>

Goal: Finding the balance point of the bow and doing the Seesaw exercise on the bow

What To Do:

1) Take hold of the stick near the middle of the bow with your left hand, being careful not to touch the hair. With the frog toward the right side of your body, extend the index finger of your right hand and set the bow on your finger, sliding the bow to a point where it will balance. You will notice that because of the weight of the frog, you will not be balancing the bow at the middle of the stick; rather, you will be off-center, with your finger closer to the frog end of the bow. You have now found the balance point of the bow.

2) Set your bow hold on the stick at the balance point. Do the seesaw exercise that you did with the pencil, but now, do it with the bow. Your pinky and first finger will have a bit more to handle now.

Goal: Setting the left hand from standing rest position & bowing the first finger on the A and D strings

What To Do:

1) Play the Mississippi Stop Stop rhythm on the A string as you did in Lesson 4.

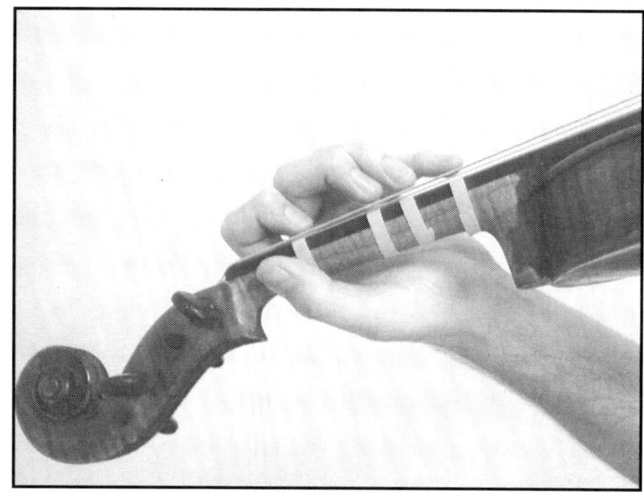

2) Take your hand off the upper bout of the viola and slide it back into playing position. Be sure all your fingers hover over the strings in a "functional position." Do not let your fingers curl under the neck of the viola or stick up in the air. Keep them in a "rainbow" shape, hovering over the fingerboard. This is the same position you learned in Lesson 3 but without the preparatory steps.

3) Bend the index finger (first finger) of your left hand and place the tip of the finger on the A string on the tape or at a place that will produce the note B. Press the finger with just enough weight to make the string touch the fingerboard. You do not need to squeeze or press too hard. The first and second joint of your first finger will create a flat little "table top." The creases of your first finger will resemble the letter "Y."

4) Play the Mississippi Stop Stop rhythm.
YOU JUST BOWED YOUR FIRST FINGERED NOTE. CONGRATULATIONS!

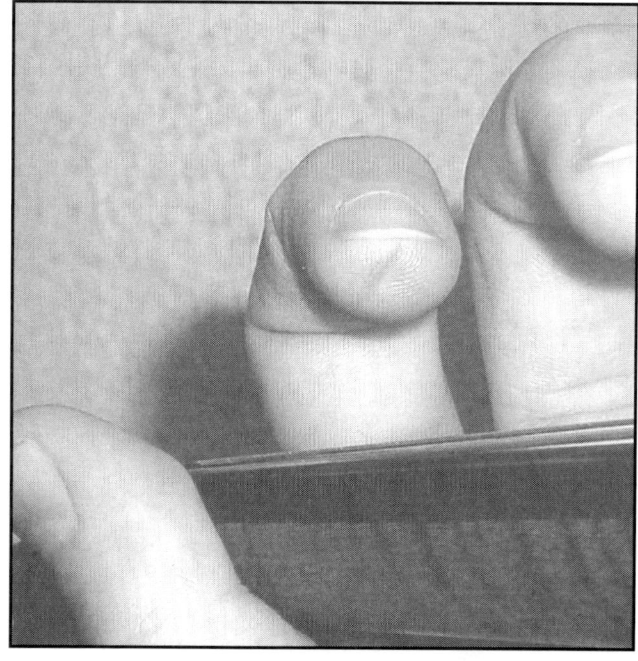

5) Lift your finger and look at the line on the finger tip. This imprint is very important, because you will want to place that finger in exactly the same place on each string.

6) Pick up the finger and move it to the D string by slightly swinging your left elbow toward the front of your body. Swinging your elbow lets your arm "deliver" your hand to the D string. Now your hand will be in position to land in exactly the same imprint on your finger. If you very gently rub the finger tip across the top of the D string you will feel the imprint or groove in your finger tip that you created on the A string. Place your finger exactly in that imprint. Play the Mississippi Stop Stop rhythm.

Music Literacy:

Goal: Placing open strings on the staff

Definition:

Ledger line - A little piece of "staff" that is added when a note sits below or above the regular staff.

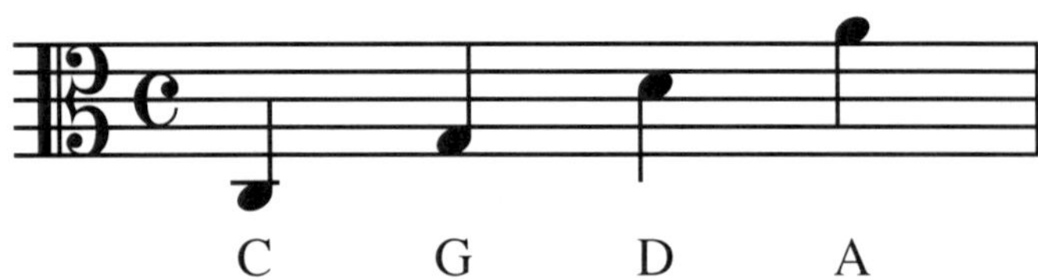

Quarter notes are placed on the staff above that correspond to the open strings of the viola. Note that the lowest pitched string, C, is literally placed "low" compared to the staff. It is so low that we need an extra ledger line below the staff.

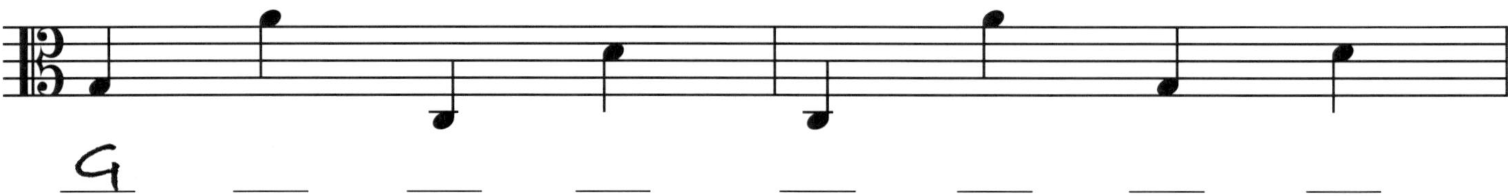

What To Do:

1) Use your hand or a piece of paper to cover the staff identifying the open string names.

2) Write the names of the open strings on the lines.

Goal: Line notes and space notes

Definition:

Space note - a note that sits between the lines of the staff. The notehead fills the entire space between the lines.

Line note - a note that sits on a line of the staff. The note head of a line note is the same size as a space note.

The note indicating the first finger is written with a line note right above the open string space note. The note name is the next note in the musical alphabet (see Lesson 1):

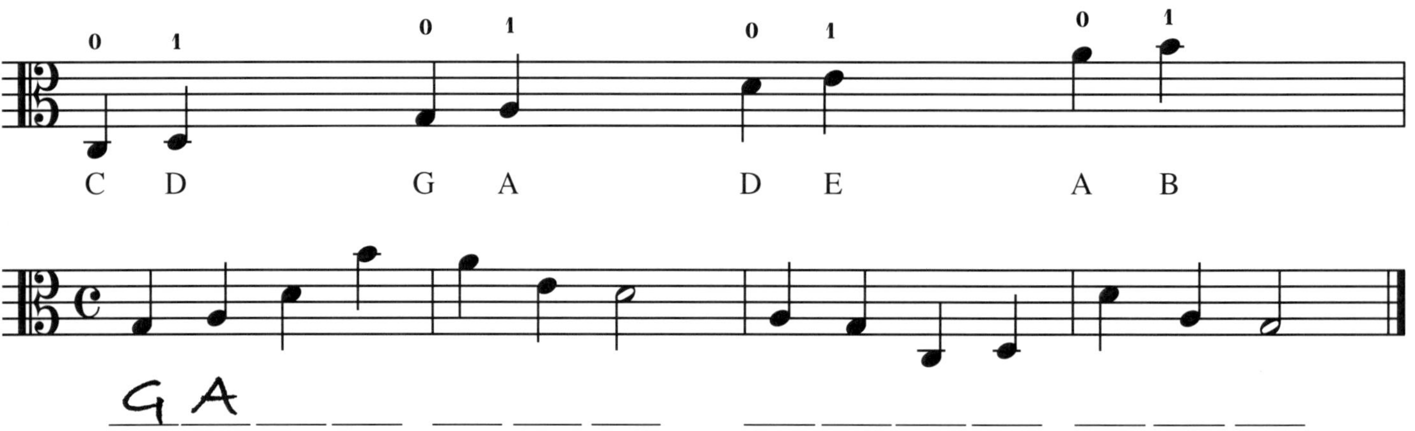

What To Do:

1) Use your hand or a piece of paper to cover the staff with the names of the open and first finger notes.

2) Write the note names on the lines under each note. Remember if it is a space note it has to be an open string. If it is a line note it must be a first finger.

Ear Training:
Goal: Using singing to help us learn new pieces

Tr. 15

What To Do:

1) Listen to the nursery rhyme "Mary Had a Little Lamb" on the CD, then sing along. The lyrics are:
   Ma-ry had a lit-tle lamb
   lit-tle lamb
   lit-tle lamb
   Ma-ry had a lit-tle lamb whose fleece was white as snow

2) Notice that the pitches you hear when you sing the words "Mary had" are descending followed by "A Lit-" which are ascending. Also notice the repeated notes in the first and second line during the words "little lamb." Remember that when you want to play pitches that are descending, you need to take fingers off the fingerboard and to play ascending pitches you need to put fingers on. If you know the first note of the song (the second finger on the D string), you should be able to imagine the fingering for the entire song.

3) Now try to pluck the song on the viola.

This Is Why:
Being able to think about the music we hear, and then think about which finger matches each pitch in the music, is the first step towards playing "by ear."

Tr. 16

Who's on First?

M. Norgaard & L. Scott

What To Do:

1) Listen to "Who's on First?" on the CD.

2) Set your bow hand and get into playing position. Next set your bow at the square of the arm on the A string. Make sure your right elbow is low and relaxed.

3) Play Mississippi Stop Stop on open A and first finger in the first measure above.

4) Play open and first finger with stopped quarter notes in the second measure. Stopped quarters are played with short stopped bows that sound very much like the "Stop Stop" notes in the Mississippi Stop Stop rhythm.

5) The third measure uses the Mississippi Stop Stop rhythm again and the final measure returns to stopped quarters.

Tr. 17

Who's on First?

What To Do:
Follow the same steps as above to play "Who's on First?" on the D string.

Lesson 6
Using all Four Fingers and the Bow

What You Will Learn:

Technique:	To use all four fingers on the D string playing with the bow
Music Literacy:	To place D string notes on the staff
	To write sharps and flats, the symbols for the note's "last names"
Ear Training:	To play back patterns using the open and first fingers on the D and A string
Tunes:	Au Claire De La Lune, Ode To Joy and Mary Had a Little Lamb

Technique:

Goal: Using all four fingers on the D string playing with the bow

 Tr. 18

What To Do:

1) Set your bow hand and check to be sure all the joints of your bow hand fingers are curved.

2) From standing rest position, use your left hand on the bout of the viola to get into playing position. Slide your left hand back to playing position as you did in Lesson 5, with the wrist straight and fingers hovering over the strings. Remember not to bend your thumb.

3) Bring the bow gently to the D string, landing at the square of the arm.

4) Play the Mississippi Stop Stop (MSS) rhythm on the open D string.

5) Set the first finger on the D string, the note E, and play the MSS rhythm. Hold down the first finger and add the second finger on the second finger tape, to play the note F♯.

6) Play the MSS rhythm on F♯. Set the third finger to play MSS on the note G, and the fourth finger to play MSS on the note A. Repeat MSS on the pitch A and lift fingers off one at a time, playing the MSS rhythm on each note, descending and ending on an open D string.

7) Repeat this exercise at least 10 times being careful to set the fingers in exactly the same imprint each time.

This Is Why:

It's a good idea to begin placing all the fingers of the left hand on the fingerboard as soon as possible because it helps shape the left hand playing position. Using all the fingers, especially the fourth finger, helps keep the wrist straight because it's nearly impossible to place a curved fourth finger with a collapsed wrist.

Music Literacy:
Goal: Learning sharps and flats, the symbols for the note's "last names"

Definition:
Sharp symbol (♯)- This symbol placed before a notehead, in notation or as a suffix to a note name (i.e. C♯ or F♯), specifies the raising of the pitch by a half step. You will learn about half steps in Lesson 21.

Flat Symbol (♭)- This symbol placed before a notehead in notation or as a suffix ie, B♭ or A♭, specifies the lowering of the pitch by a half step.

Accidental - a sharp, flat or natural sign written to the left of a note WITHIN the piece. The accidental alters all occurrences of that note until the end of the measure in which the accidental appears.

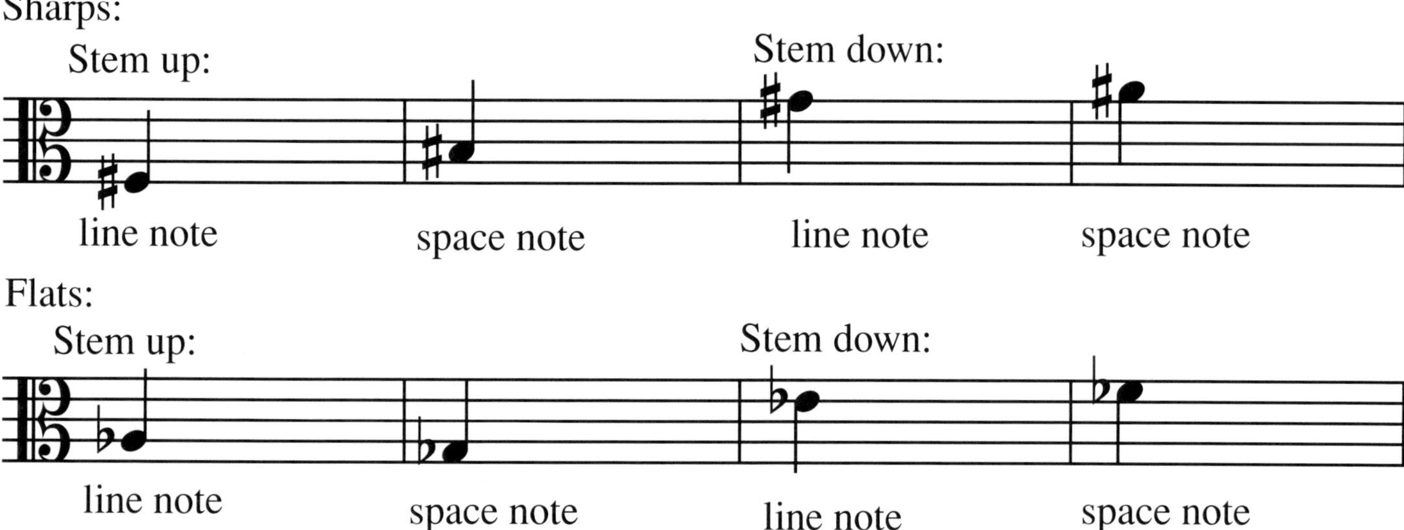

What To Do:
Copy each of the notes above. Make sure the note head and the sharp or flat sits on the same line or in the same space. Copy the stem exactly. Note that the up stems are placed to the right of the note head and the down stems to the left.

Goal: Placing the D string notes on the staff

Definition:
Scalar motion - When you recite the musical alphabet "A, B, C..." as you learned in Lesson 1, we say you move in scalar motion. As we learned in Lesson 3, you go up in scalar motion by putting adjacent fingers on the string. The notation of scalar motion moves from space note to line note, to space note, to line note...

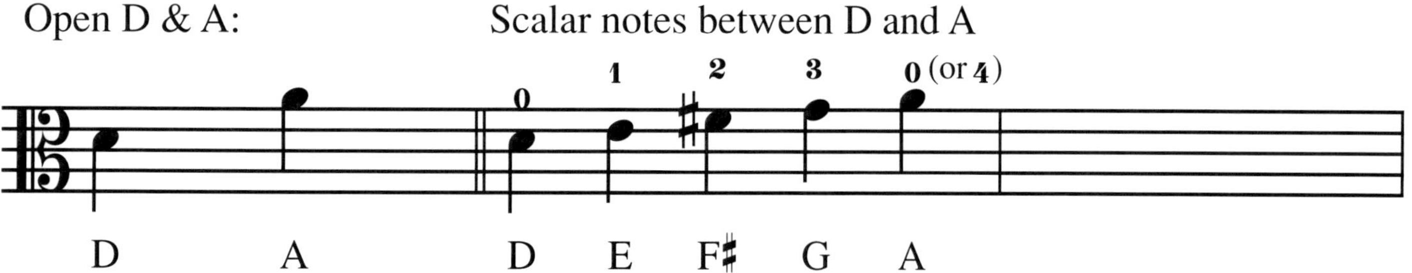

What To Do:
Copy the notes D, E, F♯, G and A in the empty measure above.

Ear Training:

Goal: To play back patterns that use open strings and first finger on D and A

Tr. 19

What to do:

1) Set your bow hold, get your viola into playing position and set the bow at the square of the arm.

2) Listen to the CD and play back the patterns you hear using your open D or A strings or your first finger on D or A (the notes you learned to play in Lesson 5).

Tr. 20

Au Claire De La Lune

French Folk Song

What To Do:

1) Set your bow hand and check to be sure all the joints of your bow hand fingers are curved. From viola rest position, use your left hand on the upper bout the viola to get into playing position. Slide your left hand back to playing position, wrist straight, thumb straight and fingers hovering over the strings.

2) Play the quarter notes with short stopped bows that sound like the last two notes in the MSS rhythm. You already played this tune pizzicato in Lesson 3, so the fingering should be very familiar.

3) After you play the open and first finger notes in measure one, leave your first finger on the string as you set the second finger.

CONGRATULATIONS, YOU JUST PLAYED YOUR FIRST FOLK TUNE WITH THE BOW!

This Is Why:

You may wonder why we use the MSS rhythm instead of the longer notes in measures 2, 4, 6 and 8. Staying in the middle of the bow and using short stopped strokes initially will help you develop good tone and bow control because your bow hand shape can stay constant. You will learn to play longer, smoother notes later in the book.

Tr. 21

Ode to Joy

L. Beethoven

What To Do:
You know the notes to "Ode to Joy" from Lesson 3. Now use your bow on these notes. Again, use short stopped bows starting from the square of the arm and remember to set only your second finger on the F♯ in measure one.

Tr. 22

Mary Had a Little Lamb

Traditional

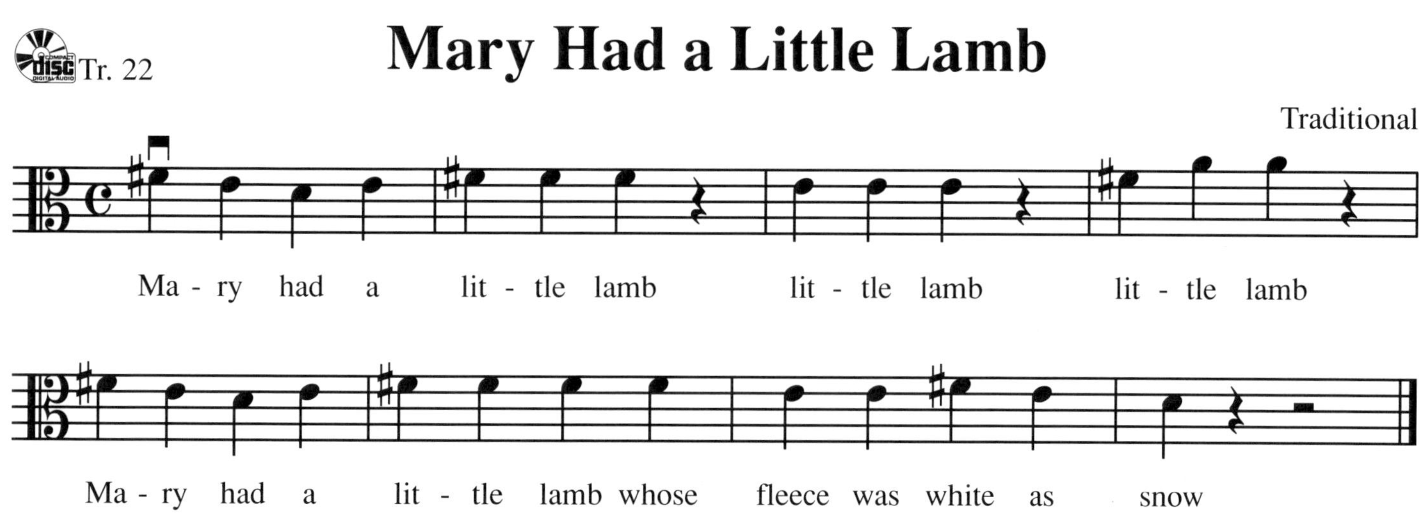

In the ear training section of Lesson 5 you may have figured out the fingering to "Mary Had A Little Lamb." It is written above in regular notation with the lyrics assigned to the corresponding notes.

What To Do:

1) Play the song from memory without looking at the music.
2) In the fourth measure set your second finger, then set your fourth finger WITHOUT putting down your third finger.
3) If you can play the song without looking at the music, we say you know the song "by ear." If you know the song by ear, you can move it to the A, G and C strings. Remember the song always starts on the second finger.

Lesson 7
Crossing Strings and Eighth Notes

What You Will Learn:

Technique: To cross from string to string and the "cher-ry pie" rhythm
Music Literacy: Eighth notes and beams
Ear Training: To play and sing the bass line to Mary Had a Little Lamb
Tunes: Rocking 'Round the Strings & The Juggler

Technique:
Goal: To cross from string to string with the bow

Tr. 23

What To Do:

1) Set your bow hand and check to be sure all the joints of your bow hand fingers are curved and put the viola in playing position.
2) Gently bring your bow to the A string and set the bow at the square of the arm.
3) Play the Mississippi Stop Stop (MSS) rhythm on the A string. You should only be using 4-6 inches of bow.
4) Now slightly raise your right hand until the bow rocks to the D string. Keep the right arm quiet and only gently move your hand to change string levels.
5) Play the MSS Rhythm on the D string.
6) Drop your elbow and your bow will rock back to the A String.
7) Now play MSS rhythm on the A string. Then rock back to D.
8) Repeat the exercise several times (the sign with the two dots at the end of the notation above means to play it twice and is called a *repeat sign*). Because you are only moving back and forth between the A string and the D string, you do not need to purposely raise the right elbow. The right elbow will raise very slightly as the bow goes from the A string to the D string.

Goal: Learn the bow direction symbol for up bow and a new rhythm

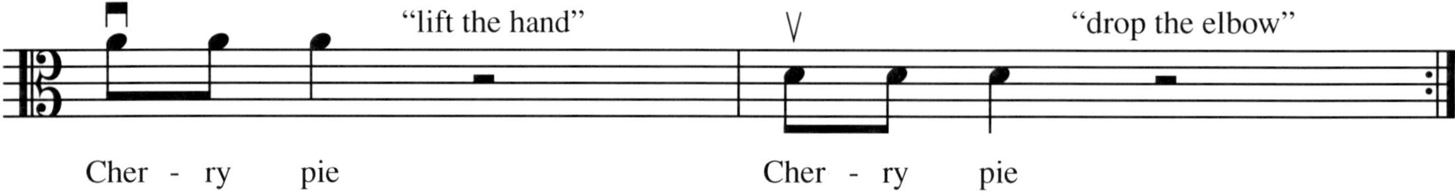

What To Do:

1) Play the string crossing exercise with a new rhythm that fits the words "cher-ry pie".
2) Notice the down bow symbol (⊓) over the first note. Your frog goes towards the floor on the first note. The second measure starts with an *up bow* marked by the symbol V. Your bow should move up toward the ceiling on the first note causing the frog to move toward your face.
3) Repeat the exercise four times.

Music Literacy:
Goal: Learning to write eighth notes with beams and flags

Definitions:

Eighth note - A note that is half the value of a quarter note. There are two eighth notes per quarter note.
Flag - A symbol used to turn a quarter note into an eighth note.
Beam - A line used to connect several eighth notes.

An individual quarter note is turned into an eighth note by adding a flag to the right side of the stem:

Multiple eighth notes are connected with a beam:

What To Do:
Copy all the eighth notes above in the space following each note(s).

Ear Training:
Goal: To sing and pluck bass lines

 Tr. 24

Mary Had a Little Lamb

Traditional

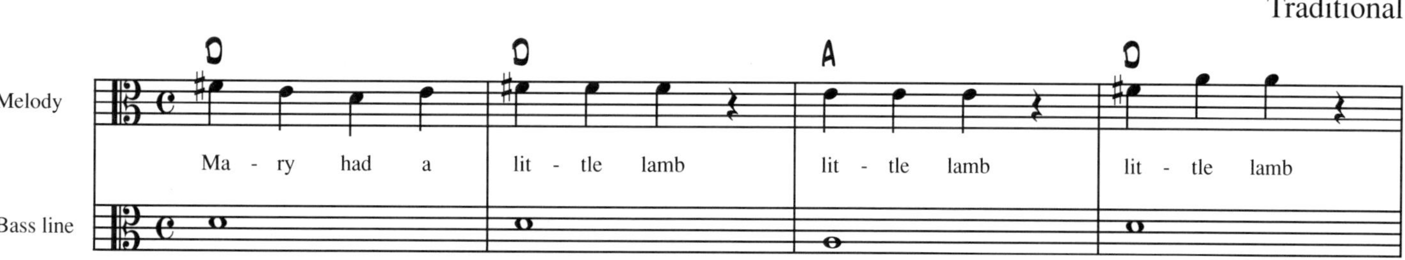

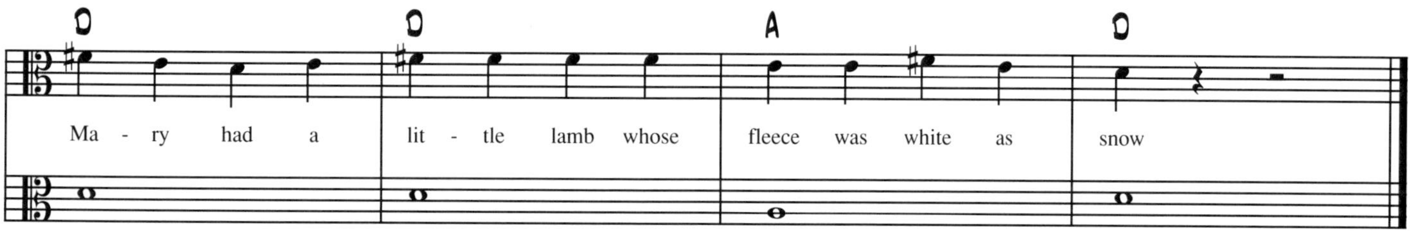

What To Do:

1) Notice that a bass line has been added to "Mary Had a Little Lamb." It is written in notation in a second staff below the melody AND notated above the melody in the form of chord symbols.
2) Sing or pluck the bass line above. If you know solfege syllables, you may call the D "do" and the A "sol."

Rocking 'Round the Strings

What To Do:
Play the piece above with stopped bows using the string crossing technique you learned earlier in the lesson. Notice it uses lots of "Cherry Pie" rhythms. The rhythm in measures 4 and 8 sounds like "Cherry Cherry Pie."

The Juggler

What To Do:
Play the piece above with short stopped bows.

Review:

These are the things you've learned about the viola so far:

1) The correct way to hold the viola and bow.
2) How to find the balance point of the bow.
3) How to set the bow at the square of the arm.
4) How to use the left hand fingers.
5) How to cross strings.

These are the things you've learned about music so far:

1) The musical alphabet uses notes from A-G.
2) When you put fingers on the string the pitches of the notes played ascend, when you take fingers off the notes descend.
3) How to use singing to help learn new pieces.
4) How to play what you hear.
5) How to sing bass lines.

These are the things you've learned about reading music so far:

1) Notes live on the five lines or the four spaces of a staff.
2) When notes are too low or too high to be represented on the staff, we add lines called ledger lines.
3) The alto clef is used for viola music.
4) When notes move up the staff the note names move *forward* through the alphabet. When notes move down the staff note names move *backward* through the alphabet .
5) Where the open strings of the viola are represented on the staff.
6) Where all the first fingers and the notes on the D string are represented on the staff.

Lesson 8
Walking and Prepared Fingers

<u>What You Will Learn:</u>

Technique:	To use walking fingers or prepared fingers
Music Literacy:	The definition of *scale* and *root*
	To read all the notes on the A string.
Ear Training:	To improvise rhythms on the open A string
Tunes:	The Dreidel Song & Kookaburra

<u>Technique:</u>

Goal: To use walking independent and prepared fingers on the D major scale

Definition:

<u>Independent Fingering</u> - refers to playing with one finger at a time on the fingerboard.

<u>Prepared Fingering</u> - refers to preparing a note that requires the 2nd, 3rd, or 4th finger by placing and holding down fingers on the fingerboard one at a time, until the desired note is reached.

<u>Walking Fingering</u> - refers to a type of independent fingering in which one finger goes down as another lifts up.

<u>Blocked Fingering</u> - refers to setting more than one finger on the fingerboard simultaneously. This technique is not recommended.

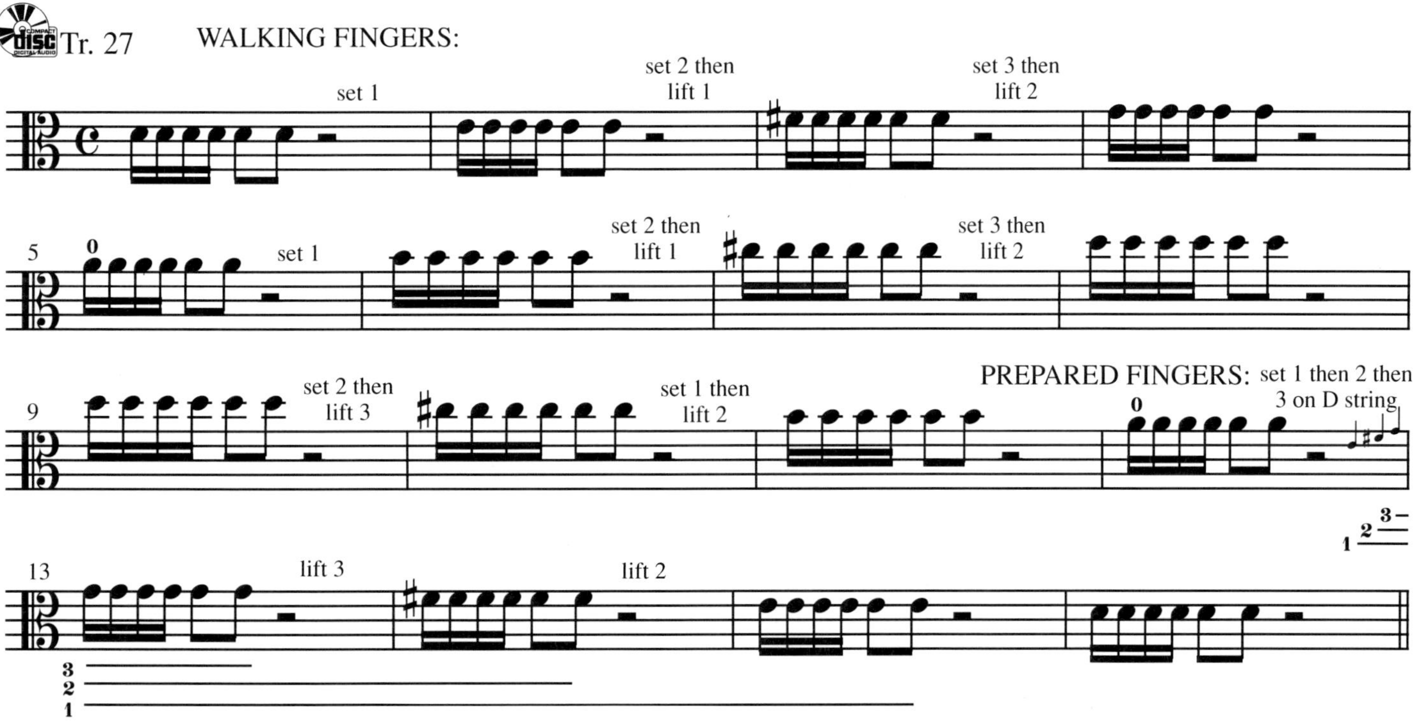

What To Do:

1) Use the rests after each MSS rhythm to place the next finger. After one finger goes down on the fingerboard, the old finger lifts up (*walking fingers* in slow motion).

2) After measure 12, (in preparation for mm. 13-16) set and hold down one finger at a time: first, second, and third fingers on the fingerboard. The lines extended under the measures indicate that you should hold fingers down for the duration of the line. You have now "prepared" the next four measures (*prepared fingers*). Lift fingers one at a time during the rests as you descend to the open D string.

This Is Why:
Speed, intonation, articulation and nearly all advanced left hand technique requires the development of *independent fingering*. For example, you will shift and vibrate with one finger on the fingerboard at a time.

Using *walking fingers* is the most efficient way to measure the distance between fingers that is compatible with advanced techniques. It is comparable to walking feet in that for an instant both feet are on the ground at the same time. Playing with walking fingers on the viola also eliminates the possibility of hearing the open string between fingered notes.

Using *prepared fingers* helps shape the left hand by allowing fingers to feel the distance of the interval between each note. Prepared fingering is used only in the beginning stages of study, until the fingers have memorized the correct left hand shape. It is very important if someone is using prepared fingering, that fingers are placed one at a time as opposed to *blocked fingering*, which means actually putting more than one finger down on the fingerboard at the same time. Putting down two or three fingers at the same time can create tension or gripping in the left hand, and may set fingers in the wrong place. Using blocked fingering will detrimentally effect intonation and all advanced left hand technique.

Music Literacy:

Goal: Placing the A string notes on the staff and scale definition

Definitions:
<u>Scale</u> - A scale is a sequence of notes in ascending or descending order of pitch. To play a scale often refers to playing the scale from root to root.

<u>Root</u> - The fundamental tone of a scale (or key or chord). For example, the root of the D major scale that you played on the previous page, is the note D.

The notes on the A string:

What To Do:
Copy the notes A, B, C♯, D and E in the empty measure.

<u>**Ear Training:**</u>
Goal: To imitate or improvise rhythms on the open A string

Tr. 28

1) Play back the rhythms on the open A string exactly as they appear on the CD. You are imitating the rhythms on the CD. You could also say the CD is asking you a musical question and that you are repeating the question.

2) Improvise rhythmic answers on the open A string. Think of the rhythms on the CD as musical questions, and rather than repeating the questions, try to answer the questions. In other words, play a new rhythm instead of the rhythm you hear on the CD. You just *improvised* your own rhythms.

Tr. 29

The Dreidel Song

Jewish Children's Song

What To Do:

1) Use independent fingers throughout the piece. For example, pick up your first finger when placing the second finger for the initial F♯ in measure 2.

2) Notice the lines that indicate a finger is held down.

Tr. 30

Kookaburra

Australian Round

What To Do:

1) In measure 2 set your second finger on the D string without putting down the first.

2) Initially prepare the third finger in measures 5 and 6 as indicated. Later review the piece placing all third fingers independently.

Lesson 9
Playing On All Strings

<u>What You Will Learn:</u>

Technique:	How the bow hold balances the bow
	To let the left arm "deliver" the hand to each string
	To use independent fingers on a new string level
Music Literacy:	To read and write the notes on the G and C strings
Ear Training:	To sing the melody and bass line to Harvest Song
Tunes:	Ode To Joy (in G and C major) & Harvest Song

<u>Technique:</u>

Goal: Letting the bow hold balance the bow

What To Do:

1) Set your bow hand and place the bow at the frog on the C string. All joints of your bow hand fingers should be curved, with your pinky sitting on top of the stick.

2) Straighten your pinky and ring finger, pushing the bow to the A string. This is similar to the seesaw exercise we did with the pencil and later at the balance point of the bow.

3) Very gently release the force on the pinky and you will feel the bow rock back to the C string.

4) Repeat this exercise, feeling the bow pivot on your thumb while you practice the "extremes" of your bow hold. You will lose and regain the shape of your bow hand as you rock to the A string and back again. Be very careful to keep your thumb bent and not let the thumb slip through the frog.

Goal: Letting the left arm "deliver" the hand to each string

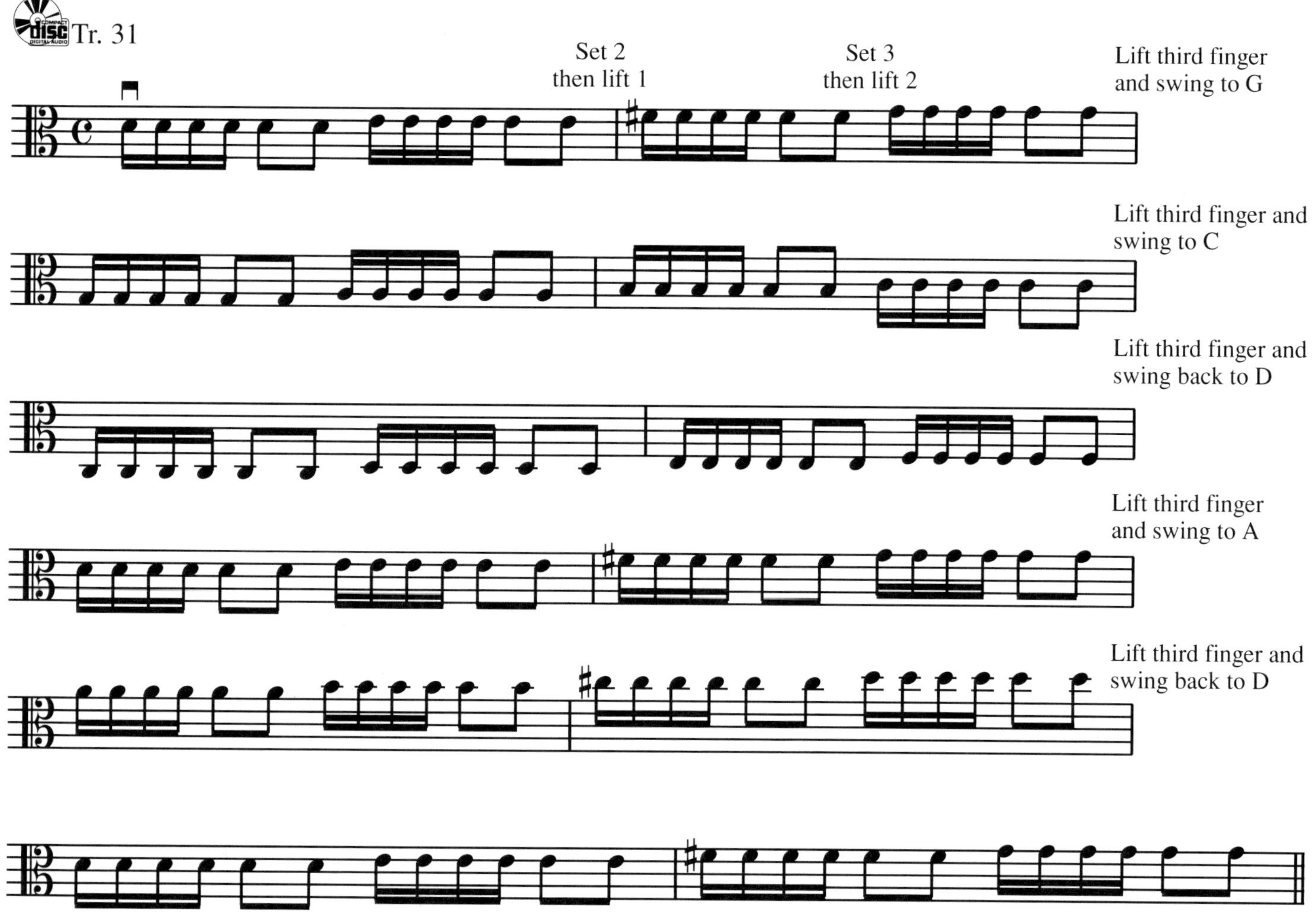

What To Do:

1) Get your viola into playing position with all four fingers hovering over the D string.
2) Play the MSS rhythm on open, first, second and third finger on the D string. Use walking fingers throughout the exercise.
3) Now lift your third finger so all the fingers are hovering above the D string (see picture on page 15).
4) Swing your left elbow toward the front of your body to "deliver" your left hand to the G string.
5) Play the MSS rhythm on open, first, second and third finger on the G string.
6) Now lift your third finger so all the fingers are hovering above the G string. If you swing your elbow a little further, your hand will hover over the C string.
7) Play the MSS rhythm on open, first, second and third finger on the C string.
8) Lift your third finger and let your elbow relax and become centered under the viola. Your arm has now "delivered" your hand back to the D string.
9) Play the MSS rhythm on open, first, second and third finger on the D string again.
10) Swing your elbow out very slightly if necessary to hover your fingers over the A string.
11) Play the MSS rhythm on open, first, second and third finger on the A string.
12) Let your elbow relax now and center it under the viola. Your arm has now "delivered" your hand back to the D string.
13) Play the MSS rhythm on open, first, second and third finger on the D string.

This Is Why:

It is very important to maintain the shape of your left hand as you move from string to string. When you maintain this shape, your fingers will fall more reliably on the fingerboard. This not only affects how well you play in tune, but will also affect advanced techniques like vibrato and shifting.

Music Literacy:

Goal: Placing the G string notes and the C string notes on the staff

The notes on the G string:

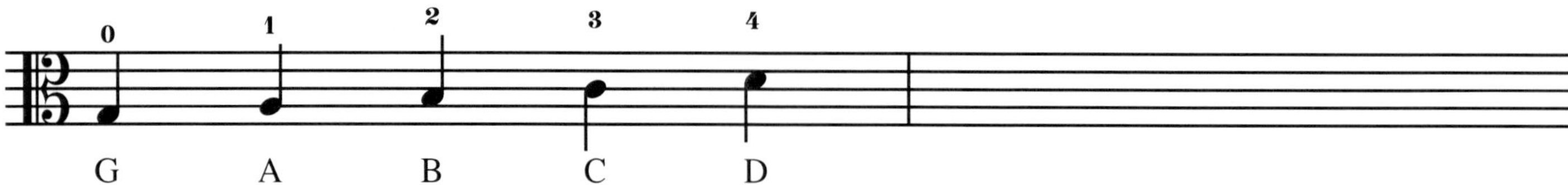

The notes on the C string:

What To Do:

1) Copy the G string notes G, A, B, C and D in the empty measure.

2) Copy the C string notes C, D, E, F and G in the empty measure.

Tr. 32

Ode to Joy

(in G major)

L. Beethoven

What To Do:

Hover your fingers over the fingerboard and gently swing your elbow so fingers are over the G string. Be sure finger imprints are centered (see picture on page 29) and your fingers are standing tall.

Tr. 33

Ode to Joy

(in C major)

L. Beethoven

What To Do:

Hover your fingers over the fingerboard and gently swing your elbow so fingers are over the C string. Use the weight of the right arm to help the bow sink into the C string for a strong sound.

Ear Training:

Goal: To sing the melody and bass line to Harvest Song

Tr. 34

What To Do:

Listen and sing along with track 34 on the CD. Try to imagine the fingering on the viola. After you learn to sing the melody, sing along with the bass line. If you know solfege syllables, you may call the G "do," the C "fa" and the D "sol."

Tr. 35

Harvest Song

Danish Folk Song

Melody

Bass line

G G Lift 3 and swing to G C G

Out in the Mead-ows the grain has been cra-dled, Rye and wheat are stacked and soon the

4 D G G G Lift 3 and swing to G

hay is in the barn. Trees have been shak - en and fruit has been gath - ered,

7 C G D G G D

home ward now we wind our way up on the fi-nal load. Glad - ness ev-ery where,

10 D G C G D G

games and dance out there; sing-ing mer-ri - ly we bind the hap-py har-vest wreath.

What To Do:

1) Play the top line above labeled "melody." You can also pluck the bass line or play it with short stopped bows. At the end of measures 2 and 6 lift the third finger slightly and swing your elbow toward the front of your body to deliver your left hand to the G string before playing the third finger on G.

2) Note the repeat signs in measures 9 and 12, indicating the measures between the signs are to be played twice.

Lesson 10
Bow Circles with Silent Landings

<u>What You Will Learn:</u>
Technique: To make bow circles and silent bow landings
Music Literacy: Finding the key of pieces by looking at the last note
Ear Training: Remembering the sound of the root throughout the song
Tunes: Roundabout & Arkansas Traveler

<u>Technique:</u>
Goal: Silent landings

What To Do:
1) Set your bow hand and put your viola into playing position. It is very important that the thumb is bent and touching the stick between the nail and fingertip. You will REALLY need the thumb to support the bow to make bow circles and to land silently!

2) Set the bow on the A string near the balance point. This is a bit closer to the frog than the square of the arm. See Lesson 5 to find the balance point.

3) Gently lift the bow "taking off" from the string about 1 or 2 inches. Feel the thumb supporting the bow and your fingers helping to balance the bow. Try to keep the tip of the bow and the frog of the bow in the same plane. In other words, support the entire bow so it doesn't feel "wobbly."

4) Land without making a sound. Because you are supporting and balancing the bow you should be able to land silently.

Goal: Bow circles with silent landings

Definition:
Bow circle (❜) - A movement you make with the bow to play two down bows (or up bows) in a row.

Tr. 36

What To Do:
1) Play a note on the A string using a down bow stroke starting at the balance point. Use about 6 inches of bow. After the stroke, make a counter-clockwise circle with the bow and land again silently at exactly the place you started the stroke.

2) Repeat the open A several times using only downbows.

3) Try bow circles on other strings.

Music Literacy:
Goal: Finding the root note and key of pieces

Definition:
Key - The key of a particular piece corresponds to the scale the notes in the piece are derived from. In all the pieces in this book you can determine the key of the piece by looking at the last note of the melody.

What To Do:
Find the key in each of the following pieces by looking at the last note of the melody: Kookaburra (page 35), Harvest Song (page 39), Sing-a-Ling-a-Ling (page 45), Wildwood Flower (page 49), Armenian Lullaby (page 53), Danish Folk Song (page 61) and St. Anthony's Chorale (page 64). Check your answers by looking at the answer key on page 81.

Ear Training:
Goal: Remembering the sound of the root throughout the song

Tr. 30 (Kookaburra track)

What To Do:
"Kookaburrra" is in the key of D, which means D is the root note (see page 40) and the last note of the song. Pluck and sing the note D to remember the sound of the pitch. Now play part of track 30 that contains the viola playing the melody to "Kookaburra." Stop the CD somewhere in the middle of the song. Can you still sing the pitch D? Check it by singing, then plucking it on the viola.

Tr. 37

Arkansas Traveler

American Fiddle Tune

What To Do:
Play "Arkansas Traveler" with independent fingers and bow circles where indicated.

Lesson 11:
Ring Tones and the 4th Finger

<u>**What You Will Learn:**</u>

Technique: How to use the 4th finger (the pinky) on the left hand
How to use ring tones to help you play in tune
Music Literacy: To write a G major scale using correct stem direction
Ear Training: To sing arpeggio patterns
Tune: Sail Away, Ladies

<u>**Technique:**</u>

Goal: To play with the 3rd and 4th finger in tune, causing the adjacent strings to ring

Definition:

<u>Ring tones</u> - fingered notes that have a ringing tone because they cause a sympathetic vibration of an open string.

Tr. 38

What To Do:

1) Place your third finger independently on the D string to play the pitch G.

2) Play the MSS rhythm on the pitch G. As you play, watch your G string. Did the G string vibrate even though you didn't touch it with your bow? The G string will "play along," making a ringing sound (*ring tone*), if you are playing the note G on the D string perfectly in tune. Listening for ring tones on your viola that make your open strings vibrate will help you play in tune.

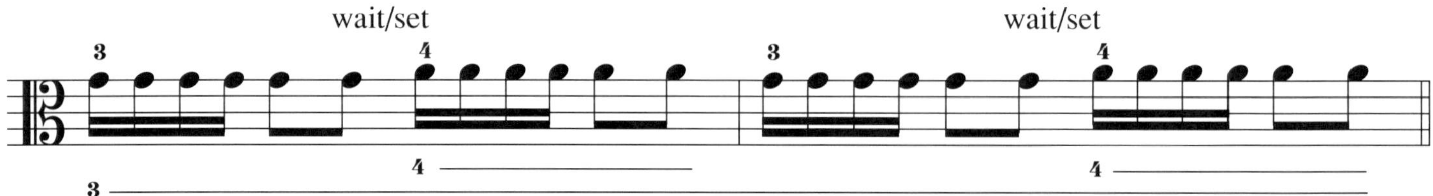

What To Do:

1) Play the MSS rhythm with the third finger on the D string listening for the G string to ring.

2) Set the 4th finger on the D string with a round 4th finger shape while keeping the third finger down. Make sure the 3rd and 4th do not touch the A string. Stand them tall and make a "tunnel" for the A string, leaving it free to vibrate.

3) Play MSS with the 4th finger on the D string. The A string will "play along" if you are playing the pitch A on the D string perfectly in tune.

This Is Why:

Ring tones help establish perfect intonation from the beginning stages of instruction. The ring tones occur because the adjacent string "rings" when the same pitch is played on another string. The exercise above helps establish perfect intonation and left-hand shape because sympathetic vibrations require the fingered notes to not come in contact with the adjacent strings. Play with tall fingers!

Music Literacy:
Goal: To write a G major scale using correct stem direction

What To Do:
1) Draw ONLY the note heads on the open staff just as they appear above.

2) Draw the stems EXACTLY as they appear above. Up until and including the note B, the stems go up. From the note C in the middle of the staff, the stems go down. Notice that when the stems go up, they are placed on the right side of the note head and when the stems go down, they are placed on the left side of the note head.

Ear Training:
Goal: To sing back arpeggio patterns

Tr. 39

What To Do:
Sing back what you hear on track 39. If you know solfege, you may be able to sing the patterns with syllables. The patterns are "do, mi, do"; "do, mi, sol"; "ti, re, sol"; "sol, fa, re"; "mi, sol, do"; "sol, mi, do."

Tr. 40

Sail Away, Ladies

Folk Song

What To Do:
1) Play the tune using open strings. Later switch and use the optional 4th finger.

2) Make the third and fourth finger notes "ring."

3) Learn the rhythm in measures 4, 8, 10, 12, 14 & 16 by listening to the CD. You will learn to read dotted rhythms in Lesson 20.

Lesson 12:
Pick-up Notes and Bow Direction

What You Will Learn:

Technique: To use independent fingers on a quarter note scale
Music Literacy: To compose with quarter notes
Ear Training: To play back scalar patterns
Tune: Sing-a-Ling-a-Ling

Technique:

Goal: To play the D major and G major scale in quarter notes (one bow per note) using independent fingering

Definition:

Strong Beats and Weak Beats - Stressed and unstressed notes within a measure. The strong beats are typically played with a down bow.

Pick-up notes - One or more notes at the end of a measure that lead to a down (strong) beat. The "up" of pick-up refers to the feeling of "up" that precedes the "down" beat or first note of the next measure.

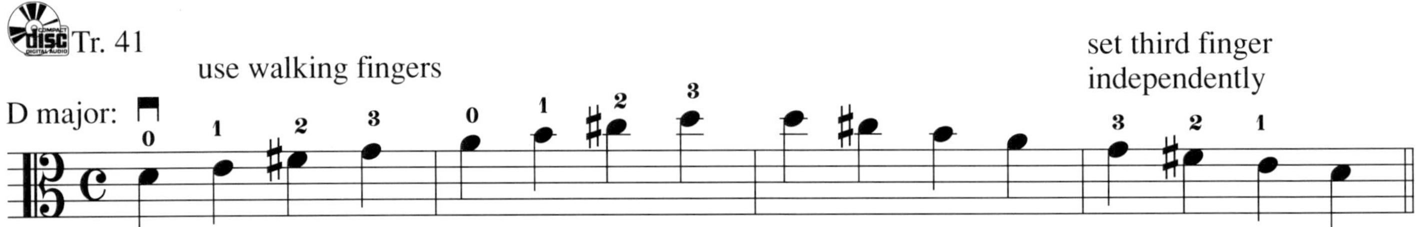

What To Do:

1) Use independent fingers to play the scale above. Each time you change bow direction, "walk" to the next note (see Lesson 8).

2) Play the scale slowly at first, then increase speed until the scale feels "easy."

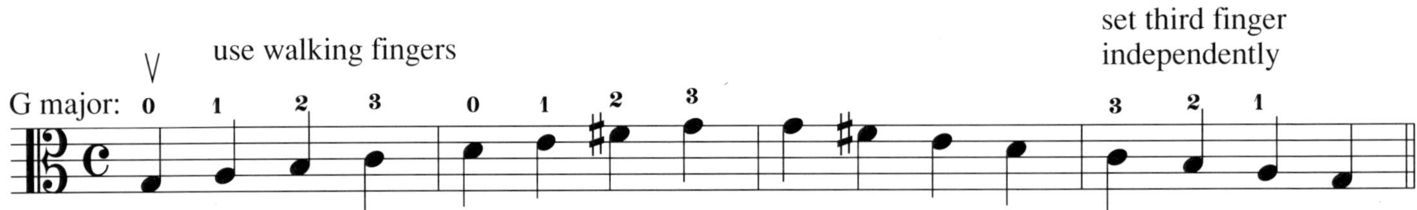

What To Do:

The G major scale starts on an up bow which may feel a bit "unnatural" (see below). Set your bow on the string in the upper half of the bow and play the G major scale starting with the bow going up. Use independent fingers on this scale also, increasing your speed as you become more confident.

This Is Why:

It is important to learn scales with all types of bowings. You have been playing long enough now that the up bow start to the scale may feel a bit unnatural. That is because most of the time down beats (strong beats) are played with down bows. Sometimes however, a piece of music may require this pattern of bowing. Always practice scales starting with both bow directions.

Music Literacy:
Goal: Compose a tune in G major

What To Do:

1) Use any of the notes you learned in Lesson 11 for your composition.
2) Compose a tune on the staff above by filling in the missing quarter notes. Each measure should have a total of 4 notes. Notice the tune starts and ends on the root G, which is also the key note of the tune.
3) Check the stem direction by comparing your composition to the notes in the scale you drew in Lesson 11.
4) Make sure to write sharps to the left of the note head if you use the note F♯ in your composition.

Ear Training:
Goal: To play back the scale patterns on the CD

Tr. 42

What To Do:
Play back the patterns on the CD. They all start on the D or A string.

Tr. 43

Sing-a-Ling-a-Ling

Folk Song

What To Do:

1) Notice that each phrase of the tune starts with an up bow marked with an V. These are the pick-up notes.
2) Listen for perfect intonation by monitoring ring tones. The ring tones G and D occur throughout the tune. Specifically in the last line, your third finger D on the A string should match the open D perfectly.

Lesson 13: Longer Bows and the Legato Bow Stroke

What You Will Learn:

Technique: To connect notes using longer legato bow strokes
Music Literacy: To count values of whole, half and quarter notes
Ear Training: To sing back arpeggio patterns
Tune: Old MacDonald Had a Farm

Technique:

Goal: To play the D major, G major and C major scales using staccato and legato strokes

Tr. 44

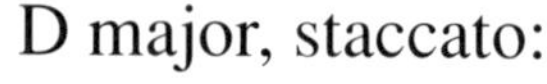
D major, staccato:

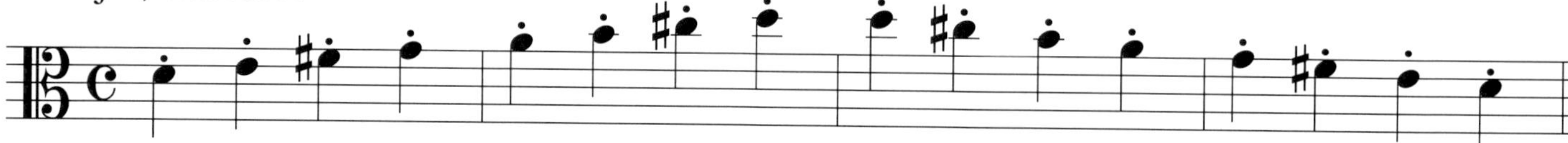

G major, legato:

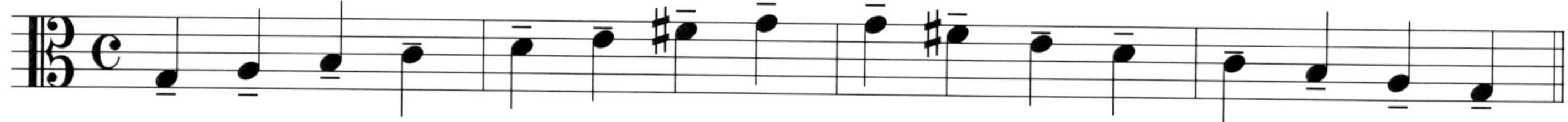

C major, you choose the articulation:

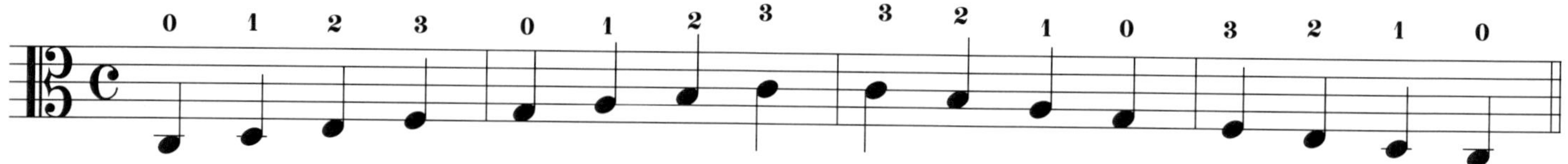

What To Do:

1) Play the scales above using the same fingerings as in Lesson 12. Notice that the new scale, C major, uses exactly the same fingering as the D and G major scales, but starts on the open C string.

2) The dots under the notes in the D major scale indicate a *staccato* stroke (short, stopped bows). This is the type of bow stroke we have used in the book so far.

3) The lines under the notes of the G major scale indicate a *legato* stroke (connected). Play each note using the middle third of the bow. The notes should sound connected.

4) Play all three scales both staccato and legato. Start the scales with either a down bow or an up bow.

This Is Why:

Music, like speech, is made up of short and long sounds, much like vowels and consonants. The ability to start and stop the bow, and to play short or connected bow strokes, gives us a command over our musical language. The goal is to develop skills that will allow you to perform the style, speed, or character of any piece of music.

Music Literacy:

Goal: Place quarter, half and whole notes correctly in the measure

What To Do:

1) Each measure above contains four beats. The symbol **C** (common time) is another way to indicate that there are four quarter notes in each measure, or something that equals four quarter notes.

2) Write rhythms in each of the empty measures above using quarter notes that get one beat (♩), half notes that get two beats (𝅗𝅥), or whole notes that get four beats (𝅝). The value of the notes you choose should equal, but not exceed, four beats per measure.

3) Place each note above the correct line. For example, a half note gets two beats so it takes up the line it is placed above and the following line. Note: You should not put a half note on beat four! Since a whole note has four beats it takes up an entire measure. Which line would you use for a whole note?

Ear Training

Goal: To sing back arpeggio patterns

What To Do:

Sing back what you hear on track 45. If you know solfege you may be able to sing the patterns with syllables. The patterns are "do, mi, do"; "do, mi, sol"; "ti, re, sol"; "sol, fa, re"; "mi, sol, do"; "do, fa, la"; "sol, mi, do."

What To Do:

1) This tune can be played with staccato or legato bow strokes. Try stopping your bow on all of the notes except the half notes, then play the entire piece with smooth connected legato bow strokes.

2) Use independent fingers throughout the tune. For example, place the third finger by itself in the first measure.

Lesson 14:
Duple and Triple Meter

<u>What You Will Learn:</u>

Music Literacy: To understand meter, time signature and duple and triple meter
Ear Training: To recognize duple and triple meter
Tunes: French Folk Song & Wildwood Flower

<u>Music Literacy:</u>

Goal: To understand meter, time signatures, and duple and triple meter

Definition:

<u>Time signature</u> - The numbers at the beginning of the tune that tell you how many beats there are in each measure and what length of note each beat represents.

<u>Meter</u> - The repeated patterns of strong and weak beats in music. In duple meter, rhythm is "felt" in divisions of two. In triple meter, rhythm is "felt" in divisions of three.

The tunes we have played so far include various symbols at the very beginning of each tune: the treble clef, (Lesson 4) and the time signature (Lesson 2).

The most common time signatures are:
2/4 - Each measure includes two quarter notes or something that equals two quarter notes.
3/4 - Each measure includes three quarter notes or something that equals three quarter notes.
4/4 (or **C**, for Common Time) - Each measure includes four quarter notes or something that equals four quarter notes.

<u>Ear Training:</u>

Goal: To recognize duple and triple meter

Tr. 47

What To Do:

Listen to track 47. Try to count "**1** 2 **1** 2…" or "**1** 2 3 **1** 2 3 **1** 2 3". If it feels natural to count "**1** 2" the piece is probably in duple meter. If it feels better to count "**1** 2 3" then you are probably in triple meter. Check your answers on page 81.

Though related, the time signature of a tune and the meter of the tune are independent. You may not be able to determine the meter from just looking at the time signature without hearing or playing the tune.

French Folk Song

Tr. 48

Folk Song

What To Do:

1) Listen to the tune on the CD. Listen for the strong beats. Do you think this piece is in duple or triple meter?

2) Use independent fingers throughout the tune.

Wildwood Flower

Tr. 49

Folk Song

What To Do:

1) Listen to the tune on the CD. Listen for the strong beats. Do you think this piece is in duple or triple meter?

2) Make your own decisions about fingering for this piece. If you hold fingers down, be sure to have a logical reason (like coming right back to the same note).

Lesson 15:
Double Stops

What You Will Learn:
Technique: To play double stops
Ear Training: To play back rhythms in duple and triple meter
Music Literacy: To place half and quarter notes in 3/4 measures
Tune: Bile Them Cabbages Down

Technique:
Goal: To play double stops

Tr. 50

What To Do:

1) Balance your bow so it touches both the A and the D strings. Just because you are playing two notes doesn't mean you need to press twice as hard! Think more about balance than weight.
2) Play the notes in the first measure. You will hear two pitches at the same time.
3) Use the rest at the end of each measure to set the next finger. Make sure the finger on the D string stands tall and does not touch the A string. Leave a "tunnel" for the A string so it can ring clearly.
4) Play the second measure. Could you still hear the A string clearly? If not, you may need to adjust your left hand position.
5) Continue with the second and third fingers.

This Is Why:
Playing double stops is a great way to make sure your fingers are standing tall. Learning to balance the bow on two strings will be necessary for professional tuning and playing double stops and chords.

Ear Training:
Goal: To play back rhythms in duple and triple meter

Tr. 51

What To Do:
Play back the rhythms on the CD on the open A string. Note that some rhythm patterns are in duple meter and some are in triple meter.

Music Literacy:
Goal: Place quarter and half notes correctly in each measure

What To Do

1) Each measure above contains three beats. Because the time signature says 3/4, there should be three quarter notes or something that equals three quarter notes in each measure.
2) Write rhythms in each of the empty measures above using quarter notes and half notes.
3) Place each note above the correct line. For example, a half note gets two beats so it takes up the line it is placed above and the following line. Note, you can not put a half note on beat three!

Tr. 52

Bile Them Cabbages Down

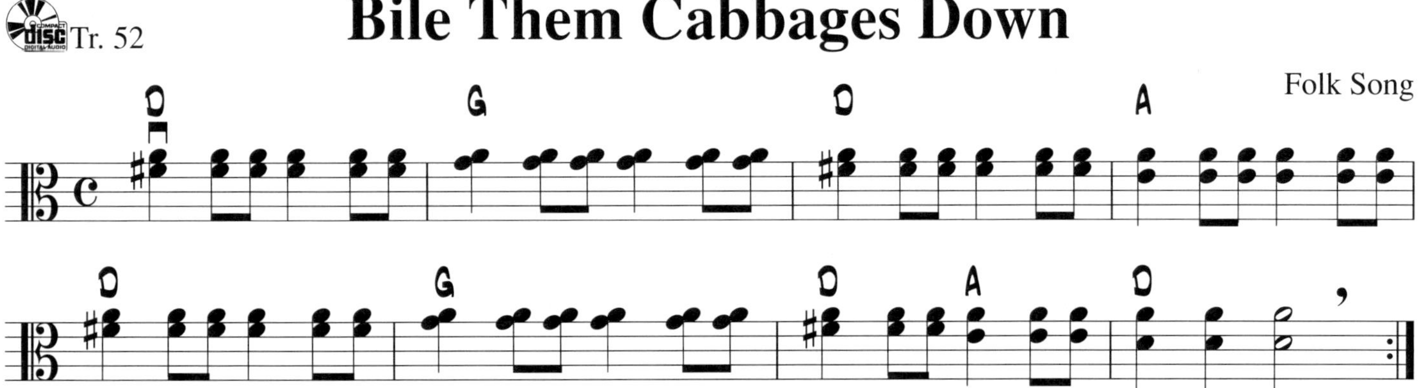

What To Do:

1) Listen to the tune on the CD.
2) Play just the fingered notes (the notes on the D string) the first time you play the tune.
3) Now balance the bow on both strings and play double stops. Remember to think about balance and not weight.

Tr. 53

Bile Them Cabbages Down (in G)

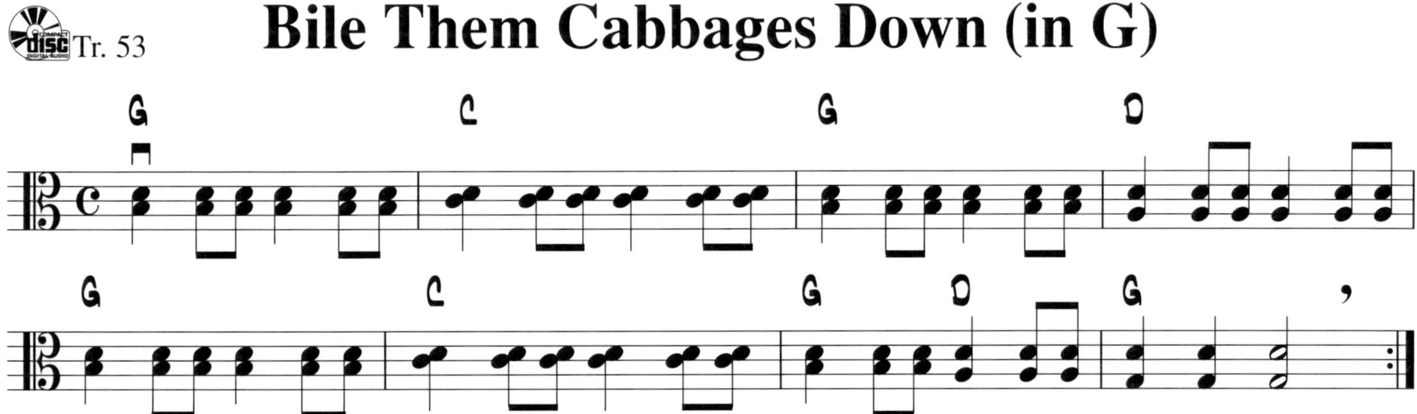

What To Do:

1) Play the tune on the G and D strings following the same steps as above.
2) Notice in both versions the chord symbols are written above the staff. You can use those symbols as a bass line. Simply pluck the pitches as they appear on top of the melody line.

Lesson 16:
Finger Hops and Key Signatures

What You Will Learn:

Technique: To hop the same finger from string to string
Music Literacy: Key signatures
Ear Training: To recognize the octave interval by ear (aurally)
Tunes: Ach Du Lieber Augustine & Armenian Lullaby

Technique:

Goal: To hop a finger laterally from string to adjacent string, landing in the same imprint

What To Do:

1) Play the first six notes of the exercise above and STOP.
2) Lift up your first finger B, and hop the finger to the D string to play the note E. You just moved your finger laterally from the note B to E.
3) Play the rest of the exercise above hopping the finger from string to string always landing in the same imprint: lift, hop, and land.

Music Literacy:

Goal: To understand the relationship between key signatures and accidentals

Definition:

Accidental - a sharp, flat or natural sign written to the left of a note WITHIN the piece. The accidental alters all occurrences of that note until the end of the measure in which the accidental appears.
Key signature - the sharps or flats at the beginning of the piece. These sharps and flats apply to all occurances of the corresponding notes throughout the entire tune.

D major scale notated with accidentals

D major scale notated with the accidentals moved to create the D major key signature

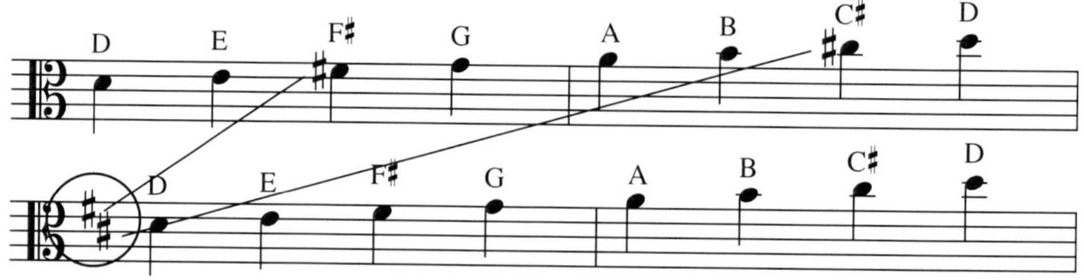

Notice that the note names in both scales listed above are the same. The accidentals in the scale are moved to create the key signature in the second example.

What To Do:

Copy each of the key signatures into the empty measures.

Ear Training:
Goal: To recognize the octave aurally

Definition:
Octave - the interval between two notes eight scale steps apart. The two notes will have the same name.

Tr. 55

What To Do:
Write the numbers 1-8 on a piece of paper then listen to track 55. The track consists of eight pairs of notes followed by a pause. If you think the pair of notes sound very similar, the interval is probably an octave. Write "octave" next to the number if you think the two notes are an octave apart. If you think the interval is NOT an octave just write "no." You can check your answers on page 81.

Tr. 56

Ach Du Lieber Augustine

German Song

What To Do:
1) Make sure you hop your first finger from the D string to the G string in bars 3, 7, 9, 11 and 15.
2) Learn the dotted rhythm in measures 1, 5 & 13 by listening to the CD.

What To Do:
1) Make sure you hop the second finger from the D string to the G string in bars 1, 2 and 6.
2) In the end of measure 6, stop and silently rock your bow to the A string for the note B.

Lesson 17:
Counting While Playing and the 6/8 Time Signature

What You Will Learn:

Technique: To play and count simultaneously
To play triplets using accented notes

Music Literacy: To "feel" music in duple that is written in the 6/8 time signature

Tune: Paddy Whack

Technique:

Goal: To play accents and count simultaneously

Definition:

Accent - Stress on a particular note. Accents are written with > placed over or under the notehead.

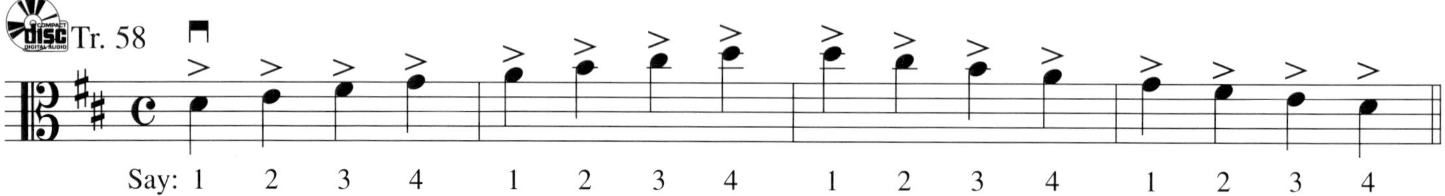

What To Do:

Play the scale above with an accent on each note while counting the beats in each measure. To play an accent, move the bow a little faster at the beginning of the bow stroke.

Say: 1 and 2 and 3 and 4 and 1 and 2 and 3 and 4 and (continue)

What To Do:

Play the scale above with an accent on each strong beat. The strong beats occur when you say the beat number and play a down bow. When you say "and" you will play an up bow (corresponding to the *up beats*).

Goal: To play triplets using accented notes

Definition:

Triplet - groupings of three notes played in the time of 2 notes of the same value. For example, a triplet of eighth notes is equal to two eighth notes.Triplets are written with a "3" near the beam.

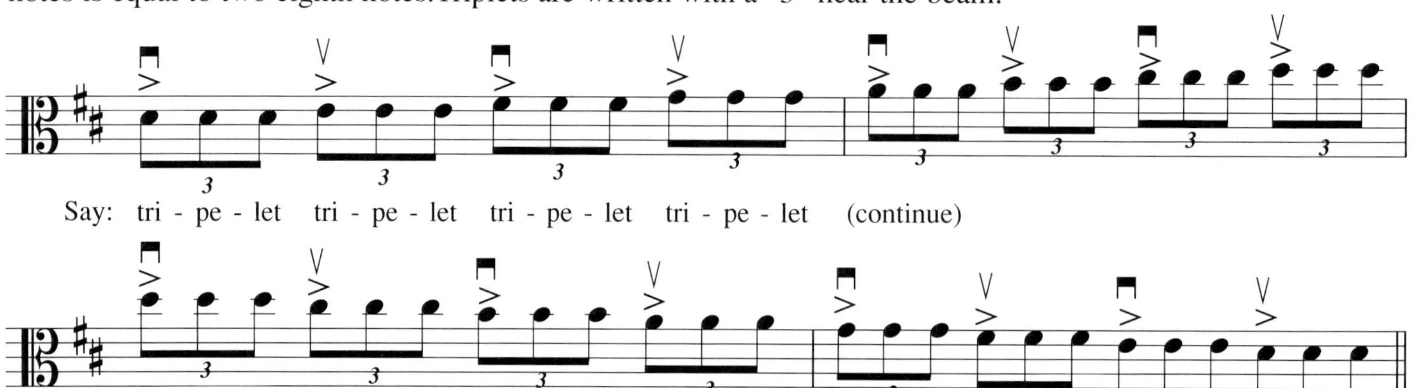

What To Do:

1) Play the scale above with an accent on each strong beat. The strong beats occur when you say "tri" in "tri-pe-let."
2) Notice the first accent is on a down bow but the second accent is on an up bow. The accents correspond to the beats of the measure. Beats 1 and 3 start on a down bow but beats 2 and 4 start on an up bow.

Music Literacy:

Goal: To "feel" music in duple that is written in the 6/8 time signature

As you learned in Lesson 14, the time or meter signature tells you how many beats there are per measure and what each beat represents. The song "Paddy Whack" below is written in 6/8. That means there are six

eighth notes or something that equals six eighth notes in each measure. You could count six beats per measure or you could say "tri-pe-let" twice.

If you play the tune in a faster tempo, it is awkward to count to 6 in each measure. Instead we count in duple as if each measure consisted of two triplets.

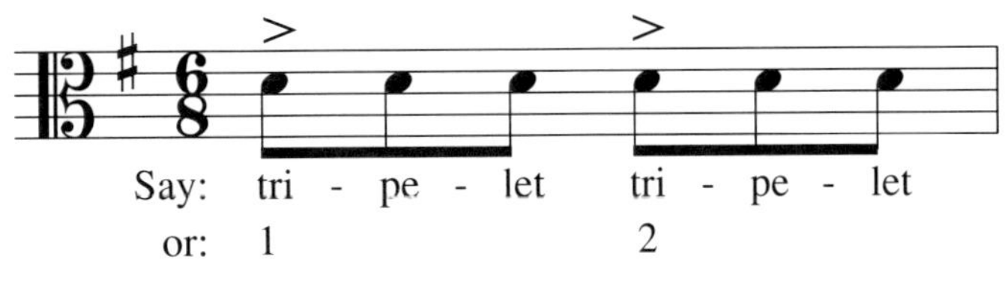

Tr. 59 (slow counting 6)

Tr. 60 (fast counting 2)

Paddy Whack

What To Do:

1) Listen to the tune on the CD. Each section of the tune is played twice. The first time you play the first ending, the second time you SKIP the first ending and play the second ending.

2) Make sure you start the tune with an up bow.

3) In measures 8, 9, 11, 13 and 17 you have to play two up bows in a row. Simply stop your bow after the first up bow and play the following note with another up bow starting where you just stopped.

4) When you play to the faster track, add slight accents to the first and fourth note in each measure. These accents will be on alternating down and up bows just like the exercise on the previous page.

Lesson 18:
Octave Harmonics and Rests

<u>What You Will Learn:</u>
Technique: To shift the left hand up the fingerboard to play the octave harmonic
Music Literacy: Rests and their relationship to notes
Ear Training: To recognize octaves and fifths aurally
Tunes: Awesome Octaves & Wildwood Flower harmony part

<u>Technique:</u>
Goal: To play the octave harmonic with perfect hand shape
Definition:
<u>Harmonic</u> - A sound that is produced by dividing the string into simple divisions (1/2; 1/3; 1/4) by touching the string lightly. It is notated with both a 0 and 4 fingering. Here are the four octave hamonics in notation:

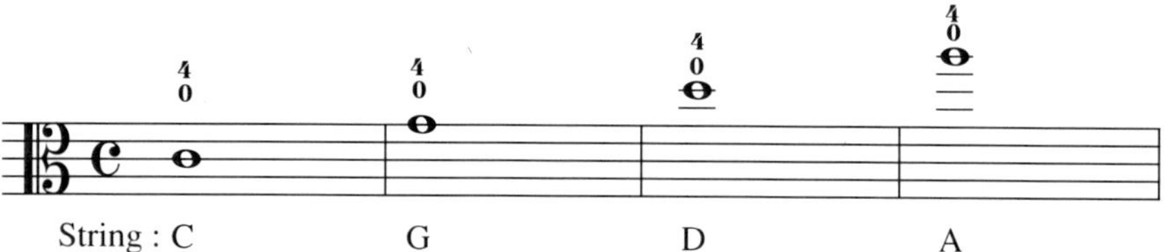

What To Do:

1) Bow an open string while touching the string very lightly with your fourth finger. Then slide the finger toward the bridge until you hear a clear "flute-like" sound. This sound occurs half-way up the string and is called the *octave harmonic*.

2) Your left hand shape should look the same as when you play in first position. Pay close attention to the "landing spot" for the thumb. The target for the thumb is the base of the neck or "the block."

<u>Music Literacy:</u>
Goal: To understand rests and their relationship to notes
Definition:
<u>Rest</u> - A specified length of silence in music.
Spaces in music are notated with rests that represent silence equivalent to specific note values.

Quarter rest: 𝄽 ____ ____ ____ Half rest: 𝄼 ____ ____ Whole rest: 𝄻 ____ ____

What To Do:
Copy each of the rests above in the spaces above the lines.
<u>Ear Training:</u>
Goal: To aurally recognize intervals of an octave and a fifth.

Tr. 61

What To Do:
Listen to track 61. See if you can hear the difference between the octave (that you identified in Lesson 16) and the fifth (the interval between your strings). Write down your answers and check page 81 to see if you were correct.

Tr. 62

Awesome Octaves

M. Norgaard

What To Do:
Put your hand in position to play the harmonic (see picture). You can leave your hand in this position until the last measure in line one. While you are playing the last beat of measure 3 (A's), move your hand back to play the B and the E. Move the hand up again for the first part of the second line and down for the last two measures of the piece. When you move around the fingerboard, it's called "shifting." In the tune above you are shifting from what is called "first position" to "fourth position."

Tr. 63

Wildwood Flower

Folk Song
arr. M. Norgaard

Melody

Harmony

Count out loud: 1 2 1 2 1 2 1 2 continue

3

7

11

What To Do:
Play the harmony line above to Wildwood Flower (the tune you learned in Lesson 14) while you count "1 2" in each measure. Count the rests even though you are not playing. Each rest in this harmony part is equivalent to a quarter note, and like a quarter note, gets one count.

Lesson 19:
Changing Bow Speed

<u>What You Will Learn:</u>

Technique:	To adjust bow speed according to note length
Music Literacy:	How to play dotted notes
Ear Training:	To imitate and play back various scalar patterns
Tunes:	Planets Aligned & Marry the Piper Girl

<u>Technique:</u>

Goal: To play with different bow speeds

What To Do:

1) Play the scales above ascending and descending (only ascending is notated) starting on both a down and up bow.
2) The bow speed on the quarters in the top line is twice as fast as the half notes and will return the bow to the original starting point. In the second line the bow speed is twice as fast on the eighth notes.
3) As you slow down the bow speed on the half notes in the top line you will notice that you have to also change the amount of weight on the bow. A slower bow speed requires less bow weight and vice versa.
4) Despite the changing bow speed, try to play both notes with even volume by adjusting bow weight.

<u>Music Literacy:</u>

Goal: Dotted notes

Definition:

<u>Dotted notes</u> - A dot beside a note increases the value of the note by one-half the note's original value. For example, a half note (𝅗𝅥) gets two beats. The dotted half note (𝅗𝅥.) would then get two beats plus one beat (1/2 the original value) to equal three beats.

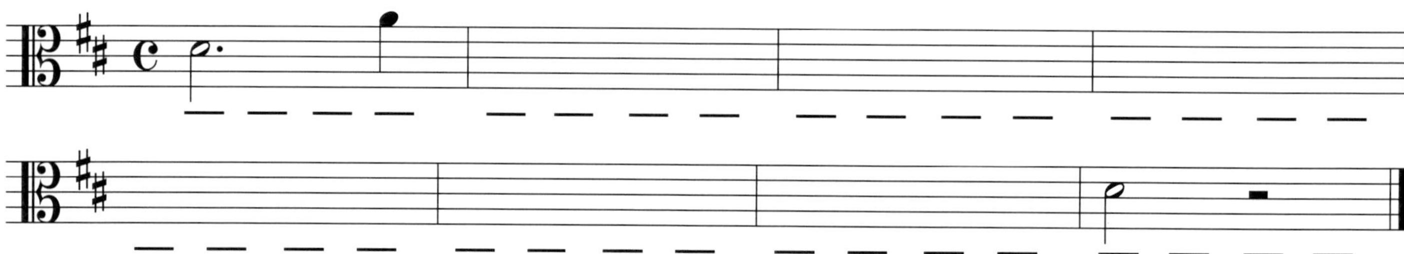

What To Do:

Finish the composition above by adding notes or rests. Place each symbol directly above the line that represents the corresponding beats. Use the following symbols for your composition:

Notes:

Rests:

<u>Ear Training:</u>

Goal: To play back scalar patterns from the key of D major

What To Do:

Play back what you hear on track 65 of the CD in the space after each figure. The figures only consist of notes from the D major scale on the D and A strings.

 Tr. 66

Planets Aligned

M. Norgaard

What To Do:
In the measures that include a half note followed by a quarter note, the bow speed on the quarters is twice as fast as the half notes and will return the bow to the original starting point. Try not to accent the quarter notes excessively even though they are played with faster bow speed.

Tr. 67

Marry the Piper Girl

Irish Folk Song

Slow count: 1 2 3 4 5 6
Fast count: 1 2

What To Do:

1) The bow speed for the eighth notes will be twice as fast as the bow speed for the quarter notes.
2) In this tune the slower bow speed quarter note is sometimes on a down bow and sometimes on an up bow.
3) The dotted quarter notes equal three eighth notes and get three counts in slow tempo and one count fast.

Lesson 20:
Slurs and Dotted Quarters

What You Will Learn:

Technique: To play two notes in the same bow stroke
Music Literacy: Dotted quarter notes
Ear Training: To improvise short figures in D major
Tunes: Danish Folk Tune & In the Bleak Midwinter

Technique:

Goal: Slurring notes of equal length with stopped or legato bows

Slurred Stopped Bows:

What To Do:

Play the first note D with a down bow, stop your bow then play the second note E with another down bow.

Slurred Legato Bows:

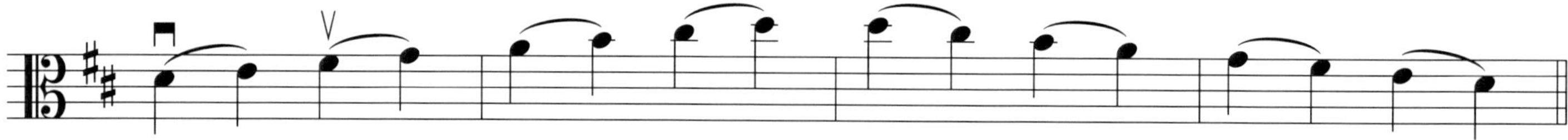

What To Do:

This time the bow is NOT stopped between notes. Play the first note D and then drop your finger to play the note E in the same down bow stroke. The left hand plays quarter notes but the bow plays a half note (changes bow directions every two beats). When you slur, your left hand makes the rhythm by changing notes. Try to "fool" the bow by putting down the fingers without the bow "noticing."

Music Literacy:

Goal: Dotted quarter notes

Definition:

Dotted quarter notes - A dot beside a note increases the value by one-half of the note's original value. A quarter note (♩) gets one count. A dotted quarter note (♩.) would then get one, plus 1/2 (half the note's original value) to be worth 1 and 1/2 counts.

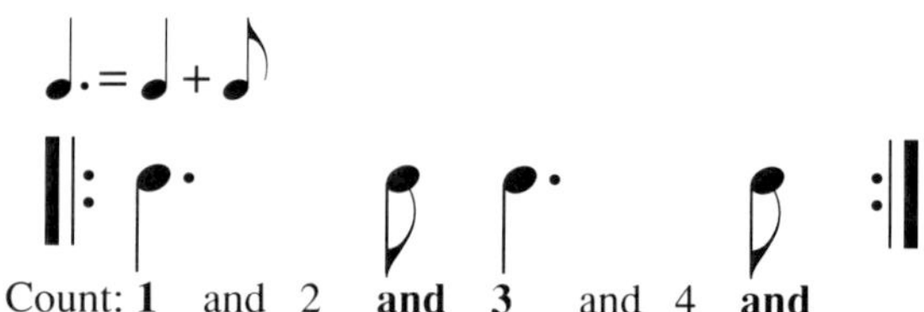

In Lesson 17 we counted the main beats and the spaces between the beats by counting "1 and 2 and 3 and 4 and" in each measure. To count the rhythm correctly, say "1 and 2" while playing the first note, then play the second note when saying the "and" between beats two and three. Clap or sing the rhythm repeatedly until you can "hear" it and "feel" it without counting.

Technique:

Goal: Slurring notes of unequal length

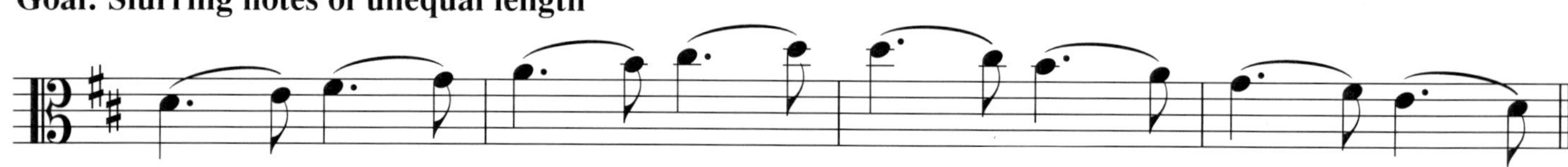

What To Do:

Play the D major scale again but this time use the dotted quarter and eighth rhythm.

Ear Training:
Goal: To improvise short melodic figures

Tr. 69

What To Do:
Track 69 consists of short melodic figures similar to the figures you copied in lesson 19. Think of these figures as musical questions. If you play back the melodic figure you heard, it is like restating a question rather than answering. In this exercise you should *answer* the musical question by playing something *other* than what you hear on the CD. You can use any of the notes from the D major scale.

Tr. 70

Danish Hymn

(Jeg ved et lille Himmerig)

N.F.S. Grundtvig

What To Do:

1) This tune is in 6/4 which means that each measure contains six quarter notes or something that equals six quarter notes. To play the rhythm precisely, count carefully allowing two beats for the half notes.
2) The symbol 𝄐 above the second note in measure 4 is called a *fermata*. It means that the note is held out longer than its written value. Usually fermata notes are held at least twice their normal value.

Tr. 71

In the Bleak Midwinter

G. Holst & C. Rossetti

What To Do:

1) This tune contains both slurred quarter notes and slurred dotted quarter and eighth note rhythms.
2) In measures 3 & 4 hold down your first finger as you set your second finger on the G string.

Lesson 21:
Low Second Finger and Scale Construction

What You Will Learn:

Technique: To play with a "low" second finger
Music Literacy: To construct a major scale using half and whole steps
Tunes: Yankee Doodle, St. Anthony's Chorale, Rigaudon & Blackberry Blossom

Technique:
Goal: To play with the 2nd finger in "low position"

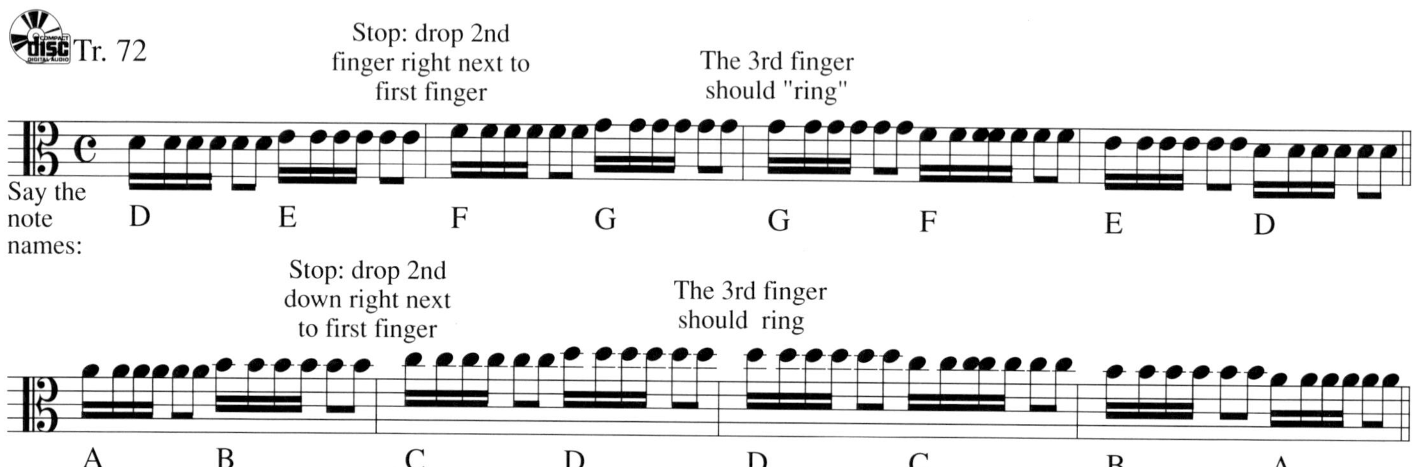

What To Do:

1) After you play the MSS rhythm on the open D string and the first finger, drop the second finger so you end up placing the finger right next to the first finger.
2) Leave both the first and the low second finger on the string. This type of fingering is called prepared fingers (see Lesson 8).
3) Set the third finger and makes sure it is in tune so it "rings."
4) Descend by lifting the fingers off one by one.
5) Repeat the exercise with walking fingers, taking each finger off the string *after* you have set the following finger. The fingers should "hover" right above the string when they are not being used.

Music Literacy:
Goal: To construct a major scale using half and whole steps

Definition:

Half step (H) - A half step is the smallest possible interval between two notes. When you play with a low second finger you create a half step between the first and second finger (e.g. the notes B and C on the A string).

Whole step (W) - A whole step contains two half steps. When you play a first finger and a high second finger (as you have in all the previous lessons up to this point) there is a whole step between the first and second finger (e.g. the notes B and C♯ on the A string).

The diagram on the right illustrates the fingerings for the G major scale. Notice that the second finger is a whole step away from the first finger on both the G and D strings. A large space between fingers represents a whole step and the notes without a space between them are a half step apart. We can write a scale using a formula of half (H) and whole (W) steps:

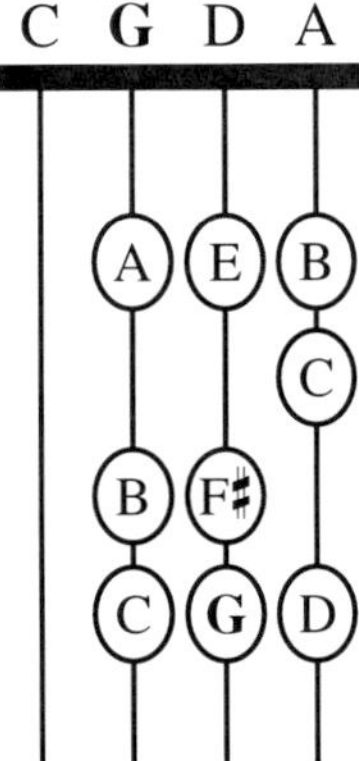

G A B C D E F♯ G
W W H W W W H

We call this combination of half and whole steps the "formula" for a major scale because it works on ALL major scales.

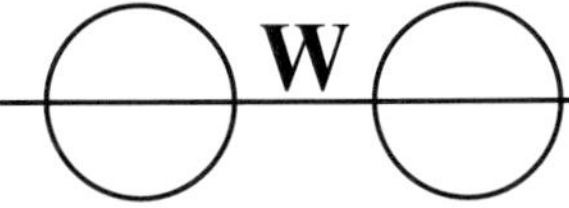

What To Do:

1) Imagine the line above is a string and the first two circles represent the notes of a major scale.
2) Finish the scale by drawing notes that fit the half and whole step major scale formula. Check page 81 to see if you did it correctly.

C G D A
D A E B
F C
E B
F C G

__Technique:__
Goal: To play a two octave C major scale

Look at the fingering on the right. Notice that the regular "high-second" finger pattern is played on the two lower strings (C and G strings) and that the new "low-second" finger pattern is used on the two upper strings (D and A strings). The key signature for C major has no sharps or flats (see below) because no notes in the scale are altered (have "last names").

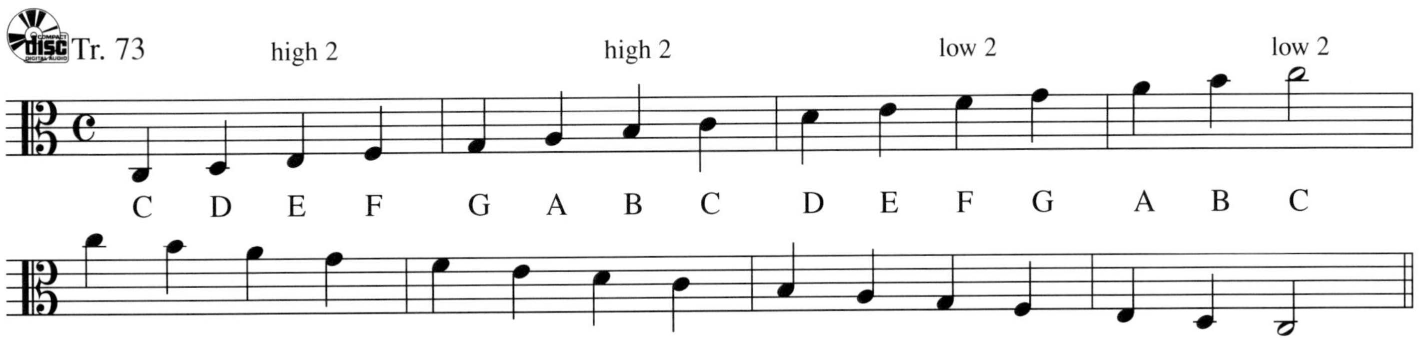

What To Do:

1) Play the C major scale as notated above using independent fingering.
2) Listen for 3rd finger ring tones on the G and D strings.
3) Also play the scale above using the MSS rhythm on each note. This rhythm gives you six chances to get every note perfectly in tune!

Tr. 73

Yankee Doodle

American Folk Tune

What To Do:
This tune is in C major. Play the tune above using a low second finger in measure 6. The slurs are played with stopped bows. You can play the bass line by reading the chord symbols.

Tr. 75

St. Anthony's Chorale

Haydn

What To Do:
This tune is in G major and uses low second finger on the A string (measures 1, 2, 4, 6, 7, 15, 16, 19 & 20) but high second finger on the D string (measures 9, 12, 13, 18 & 22). See the fingering drawing on the top of the previous page. Also note both legato and stopped slurs appear in this piece.

Tr. 76

Rigaudon

H. Purcell

What To Do:
This tune is also in G major. Watch that your third finger rings in measures 9 and 13 despite the preceding low second.

Tr. 77

Blackberry Blossom

Traditional
arr. M. Norgaard

What To Do:

1) In measures 1 and 5, set your low second finger on the A string, then play your fourth finger while leaving the low second finger on the string. This is not easy because of the big stretch between the low 2 and the 4.
2) In measures 9 and 13 you can play either open A or fourth finger. Each choice creates a challenge: crossing a string or reaching for the octave using the fourth finger.

Lesson 22:
Hooked Bows and Transposition

What You Will Learn:

Technique: To play "hooked" bows
Music Literacy: The basic principle of transposition
Tunes: The Bridge of Avignon & Scotland the Brave

Technique:

Goal: To play with "hooked" bows

Tr. 78

Definition:

Hooked bows - two notes of unequal value played in the same bow direction. The "hook" in the example below refers to the short note being "hooked" to the following note with a quick up down motion.

What To Do:

1) The rhythm on the second and fourth beats above is easiest to learn by listening to the CD. It's the same rhythm that we learned to count in Lesson 20, just twice as fast.

2) Play the first note C, then play the next note D and stop your bow.

3) Play the next D with a quick up bow that hooks to the following down bow on the note E.

4) Repeat the exercise starting on an up bow. Now the "hook" will be a down up motion.

Music Literacy:

Goal: To understand the basic principle of transposition

Definition:

Transpose - To transpose a tune means to play the same tune in another key. The tune will sound the same because the relationship between the notes is the same though the root is different.

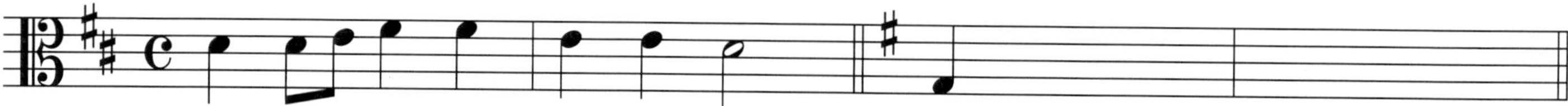

What To Do:

1) Look at the short melody above. Notice that it starts on the note D (the root) and is written in D major (2 sharps in the key signature). Also note that the tune "walks" up the scale and back down to end on D.

2) Write the exact same tune in G major using the step-wise pattern you see in the first example. Start on the note G that is written. You just transposed the tune to G major.

Tr. 79

The Bridge of Avignon

French Folk Tune

What To Do:

1) First play the tune as written in the key of G major. Note that the tune starts on the root note G. Use the G major finger pattern that you learned in Lesson 21 (high second finger on G and D and low on A).
2) Transpose the tune to C major, starting the tune on the note C on the G string. Since the tune sounds the same when it is transposed to C major, the fingering will be exactly the same, just on different strings.

Tr. 80

Scotland the Brave

Scottish March

Key of D:

5

9

13

Key of G:

Continue

Key of C:

Continue

What To Do:

1) All the dotted rhythm up bows in this piece are hooked.
2) After you can play the tune in D major, try to transpose it to G major and C major. Only the first line of each transposed version is written above.

Lesson 23:
Long Bows and Bow Hand Shapes

What You Will Learn:

Technique: To play long bows with changing hand shapes
Music Literacy: Steps and skips and the naming of intervals
Tunes: Theme from Beethoven's Violin Concerto & Marsk Stig's Daughters

Technique:

Goal: To play at the frog with a "frog hand"

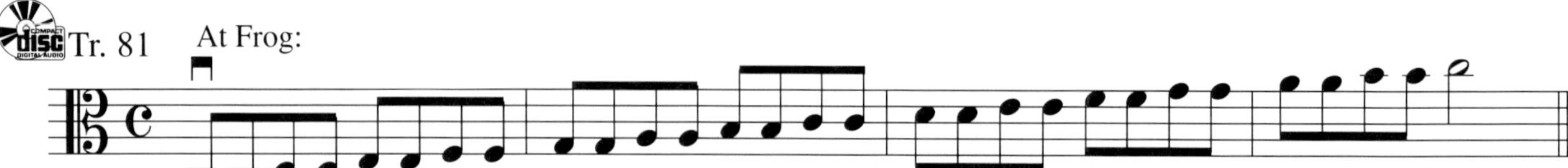

Frog Hand

What To Do:

1) Review the seesaw at the frog exercise from Lesson 5.
2) Set your bow at the frog with your pinky curled so your bow sits on the C string. This handshape is called the "frog hand." See the picture.
3) Play the scale above using short bows that only go from the frog to the balance point. Your bow hand will always be in "frog" position with all the joints completely curled.

Goal: To play long bows with changing hand shapes

Tr. 82

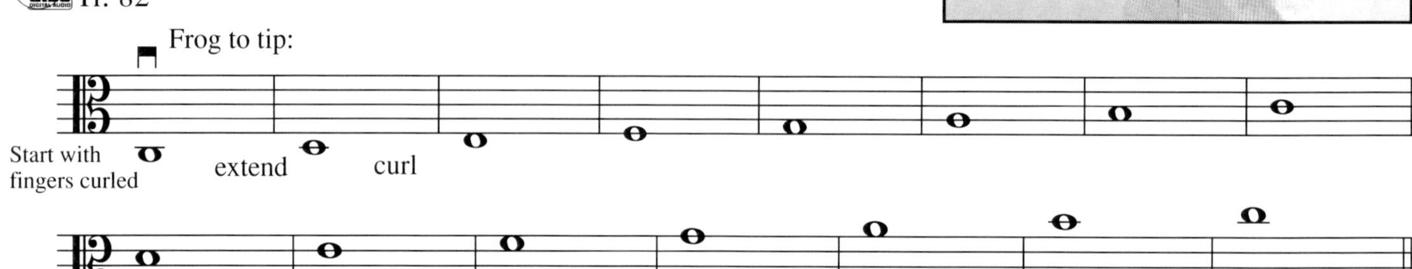

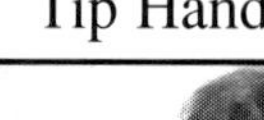

Tip Hand

What To Do:

1) Play a whole note starting from the frog. Don't worry if the beginning of the note sounds a bit scratchy.
2) Notice that as you pull the bow towards the tip, your pinky uncurls as the arm extends. Your hand is now in "tip hand" position. See the picture.
3) Change bow direction playing an up bow on the second measure and move your bow back to the frog. Make sure you go ALL THE WAY to the frog. As you pull your bow back to the frog, you should regain your "frog hand" with all joints curled. If your bow hand is flexible as described in Lessons 4 & 5, your fingers may curl automatically. If not, you may have to actively think of curling your pinky as you play the up bow.
4) Continue thinking "extend" on the down bows and "curl" on the up bows noticing the shape of the joints in your right hand.

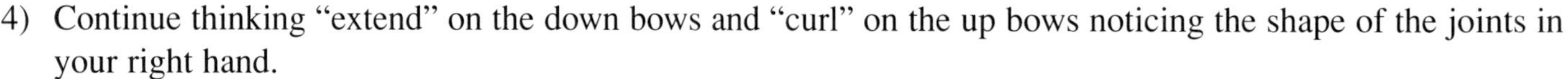

This Is Why:
The joints in your arm must bend in arcs to create a perfectly straight bow. As you extend your arm to go all the way to the tip, the fingers must follow through and straighten in order to keep the bow straight.

Goal: To use a flexible bow hand to play slurred notes on the scale

 Tr. 83

What To Do:
Play the C major scale again using slurred notes from the frog to the tip of the bow. See if you can use your new bow hand flexibility to change your hand shape from "frog hand" to "tip hand" automatically.

<u>Music Literacy:</u>
Goal: To understand the difference between skips and steps and to name intervals

Definitions:
<u>Step</u> - The interval between two adjacent notes. In Lesson 21 we defined two types of steps: the half step and the whole step.

<u>Skip</u> - An interval that is more than a step apart.

G up to A: step   F up to E:_____   G up to D:_____   C down to F:_____   C up to D:_____   B down to A:_____

What To Do:
Write either "step" or "skip" on each line following the pair of notes. If the notes are next to each other in the C major scale (see Lesson 21), they are a step apart. If you have to skip over notes to get from one to the next, it is a skip. Check your answers on page 81.

Definition:
<u>Interval names</u> - The distance between pitches is named by the number of steps you get when going up or down the scale. Include both the first and last note of the interval when counting. The most common intervals are: Unison (the same note played twice), Second (this is the same as a step), Third, Fourth, Fifth, Sixth, Seventh, Octave, Ninth, Tenth.

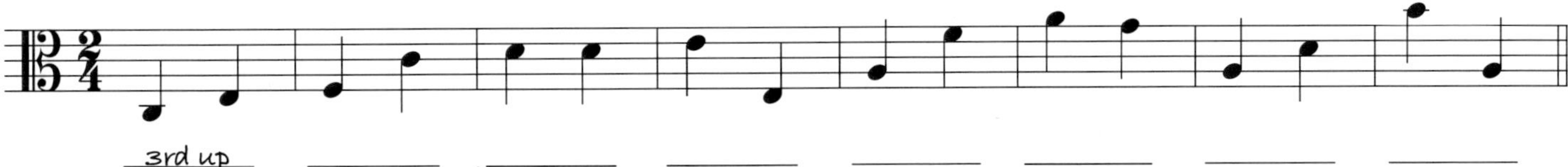

What To Do:
Write the interval name and whether the direction is up or down. Count up or down the scale to determine the interval. Remember to count both notes of the interval when counting lines and spaces. Check your answers on page 81.

Tr. 84 Theme from Beethoven's Violin Concerto

L. Beethoven

What To Do:

1) Play the theme above slowly and as legato as possible sustaining each note for the full value.

2) Your bow hand should change shape from "frog hand" to "tip hand" depending on where you are in the bow stroke.

3) Play the repeated notes with slurs and dashes by pausing the bow slightly between the notes.

4) Listen to a recording of the first movement of Beethoven's Violin Concerto in D major. The theme above is played by the winds and later with additional embellishments by the solo violin.

5) In measures 7, 8, and 13, you will see three notes connected with a slur. Similar to two-note slurs, these notes are played with the bow going in the same direction.

Tr. 85 Marsk Stig's Daughters

Danish folk tune from the Middle Ages

What To Do:

1) Use full bows throughout the tune.

2) Though the key signature is C major, the tune starts and ends on the note D. The tune is written in Dorian mode. A mode is a type of scale used in the Middle Ages.

Lesson 24:
Sixteenth Notes and Subdivision

<u>**What You Will Learn:**</u>

Technique: To play repeated and scalar 16th notes
Ear Training: To imitate small figures with steps and skips
Music Literacy: Subdivision of the beat into 2 notes and 4 notes To compose a tune in C major
Tunes: Gavotte & The Rakes of Mallow

<u>**Technique:**</u>
Goal: To play repeated and scalar 16th notes

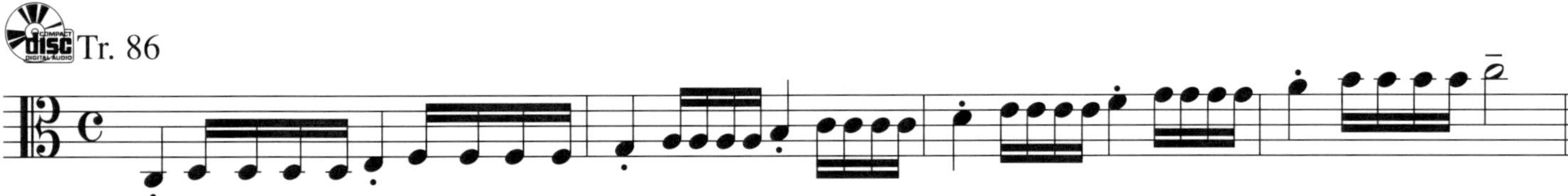

Count: 1 Mis-sis-sip-pi 3 Mis-sis-sip-pi

What To Do:

1) Play the first note C with a short stopped down bow.

2) Play the note D four times quickly while saying the word "Mississippi."

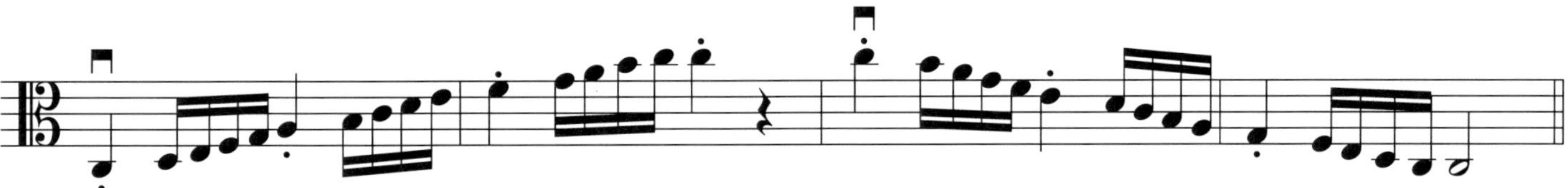

What To Do:

1) Play the first note C with a short stopped down bow.

2) Play the next four notes with very short bows. The rhythm is the same as the exercise above. The setting and lifting of your left hand fingers should be perfectly coordinated with the bow changes. Play the rhythm accurately with the bow and the fingers of the left hand should follow.

<u>**Ear Training:**</u>
Goal: To imitate and improvise with small melodic figures that include steps and skips

Tr. 87

What To Do:

<u>Imitation:</u>

1) Listen to the short melodic figures on track 87. Each figure starts on the G string and uses the notes of the C major scale.

2) Try to imitate each figure by playing exactly what you hear. It is as if you are repeating the musical "question" on the CD.

<u>Improvisation:</u>

3) Go back to the beginning of track 87. Instead of repeating the figure on the CD, answer the figure by playing something other than what is on the CD. Now you are answering the musical question on the CD. Use notes from the C major scale and incorporate skips and steps in your answers. For more information on improvisation, check out *Jazz Viola Wizard Junior Books 1* and *2* by Martin Norgaard (Mel Bay MB20188 & MB20868).

Music Literacy:

Goal: To understand the relationship between note lengths

One whole note is the same length or value as each of the following:

two half notes

four quarter notes

Possible count: 1 2 3 4

8 eighth notes

16 sixteenth notes

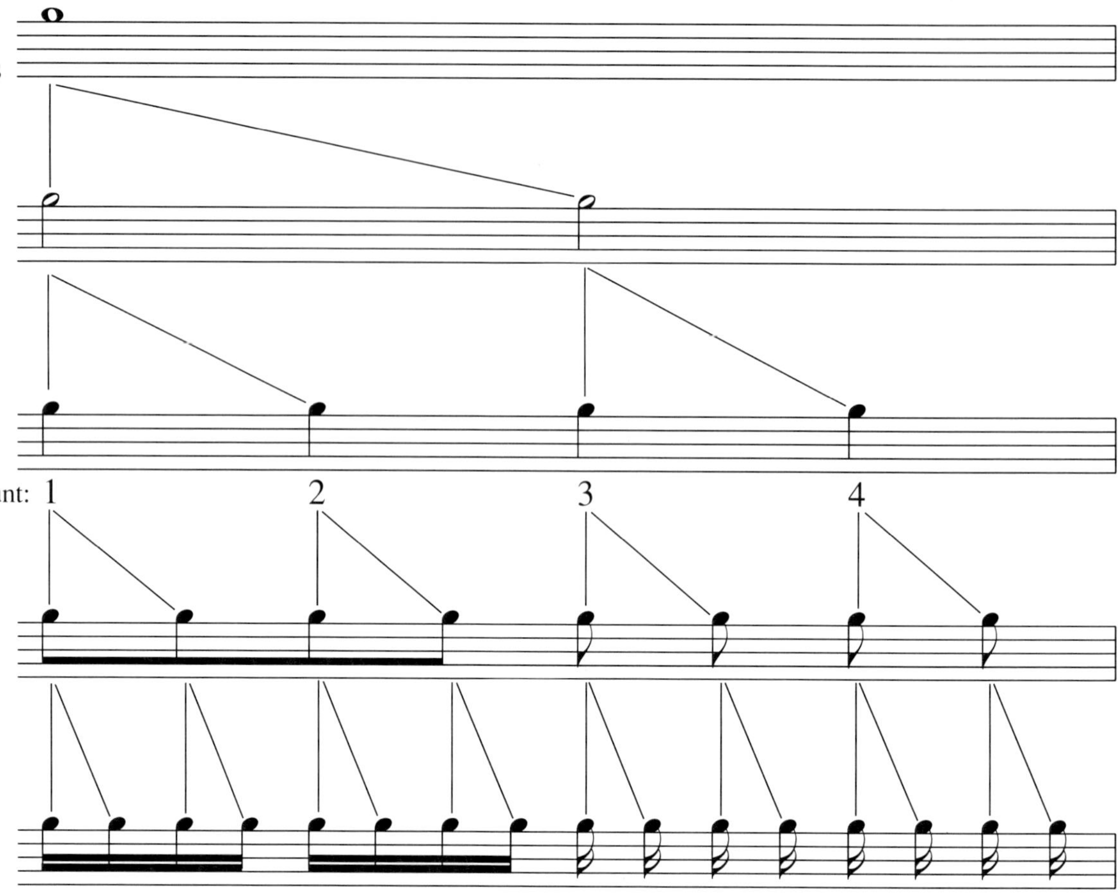

Definition:

Subdivision - A subdivision splits the main beat into equal parts. For example, a quarter note beat can be subdivided into two eighth notes (e.g. "In the Bleak Midwinter") or further divided into four sixteenth notes such as in "Scotland The Brave."

Goal: To compose a tune in C major using whole, half, quarter, eighth and sixteenth notes

What To Do:

1) Compose an eight measure tune in the space above using the notes of the C major scale.
2) For each beat (represented by a line) either use one quarter note, two eighth notes or four sixteenth notes. You can also combine beats by using half notes (two beats), dotted half (three beats) or whole notes (four beats).
3) Play the composition you just created.

 Tr. 88

Gavotte

Traditional German

What To Do:

1) Listen to the tune on the CD. Notice all the Mississippi Stop Stop rhythms. Now play the notes and try to make your left hand "keep up" with the bowing.

2) Learn both the viola 1 and 2 parts. The CD track has both voices separated into the left and right channel.

Tr. 89

The Rakes of Mallow

Irish Folk Tune

What To Do:

Listen to the tune on the CD. The left hand fingers and the bow changes should be perfectly coordinated.

Lesson 25: Low First Finger, High Third Finger and Accidentals

What You Will Learn:

Technique: To play with the first finger in "low" position and the third finger in "high" position
Music Literacy: The function of accidentals
Tunes: Slide Finger Blues, Old Joe Clark, First Western Change Jig, Son De Pedro Pineda, March & Give Me Your Hand

Technique:

Goal: To play with the 1st finger in "low" position

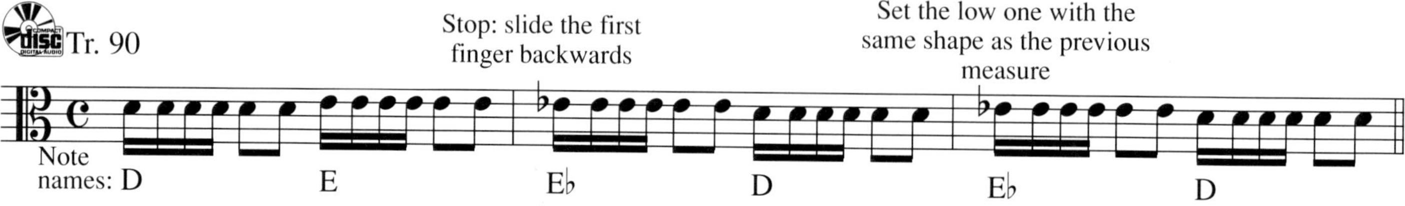

What To Do:

1) After you play the MSS rhythm on the open D string and first finger, slide the first finger backwards and play the E♭. Make sure the imprint in your finger stays the same. The creases of the low first finger will form a "Y" when viewed from the side.

2) Play the exercise above on each string. Allow your arm to deliver your hand to each string level keeping the imprint in your finger consistent.

Goal: To play with the 3rd finger in high position

What To Do:

1) After you play part of the D major scale (use high 2nd finger) and the MSS rhythm on the 4th finger, set the high 3rd right behind the 4th finger, then lift the fourth finger off. Your high 3rd should now be in tune.

2) In measure 3, slide the regular 3rd (the note G) up to make a G♯. This should be the same pitch as the G♯ in measure 2. Now put your 4th finger right next to your high 3rd finger. This fingered note A should "ring" with the open A string (see Lesson 11).

Goal: To play with low and high second fingers

What To Do:

1) After playing the open D string and the first finger, set the low second (described in Lesson 21) very close to the first finger.

2) Slide the "low" second to "high" second finger position, then slide it back to "low" second finger position.

Music Literacy:

Goal: To be able to identify accidentals with note names and fingerings

Definitions (partial review from lessons 4 and 16):

Sharp (♯) - A symbol that raises the note by a half step.

Flat (♭) - A symbol that lowers the note by a half step.

Natural sign (♮) - Negates accidentals from the key signature and resets accidentals earlier in the measure.

Accidental - A sharp, flat or natural sign written to the left of the note head within the piece. The accidental alters all occurances of the note in the measure until the end of the measure in which the accidental appears.

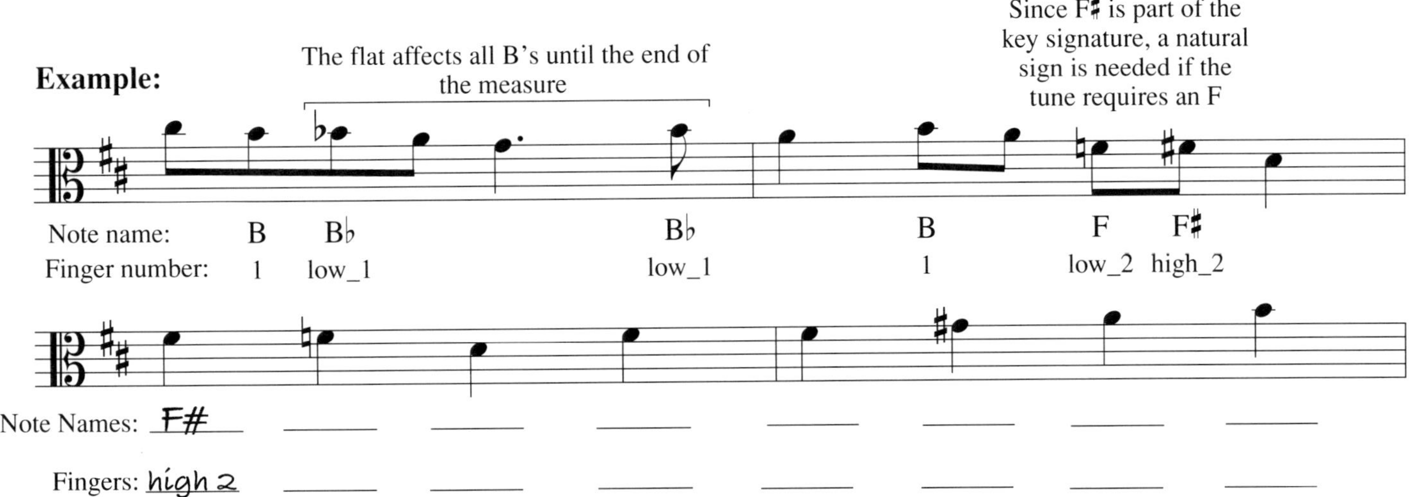

What To Do:

1) Write the note names and finger numbers on the lines as in the example above.

2) Check your answers on page 81.

Tr. 91

Slide Finger Blues

(in D major)

M. Norgaard

What To Do:

1) Review the fingerings for the D major scale (see Lessons 3 and 8).

2) Listen to the CD and notice that the eighth notes are not played evenly, they are "swung" to fit the groove. For more on swing rhythms see *Jazz Viola Wizard Junior Book 1* (Mel Bay MB20188).

3) You should hear the slide when you move from the low to the high second finger in measures 1, 2, 9 and 10.

Old Joe Clark

Tr. 92 (slow)

Tr. 93 (fast)

Traditional
arr. M. Norgaard

What To Do:

The original song is notated first, followed by the fiddle tune version. Many fiddle tunes originated from folk songs that fiddlers then developed into fiddle tunes using variations on the melodies. While many were still suitable for dancing, some were so highly developed that they turned into "concert" fiddle pieces. The current version is one out of many possible ways to play this tune.

1) Note the constant appearance of the C natural in the tune.

2) Notice the sharp in the beginning of measure 23 is not really needed. It is there to remind you to play F♯ and is referred to as a *courtesy accidental*.

3) Measures 23 and 31 use both high and low second fingers.

Tr. 94

First Western Change Jig

Traditional

What To Do:
The tune above can be counted in six or in two (see Lesson 17). It includes many high and low second fingers. After you play both sections twice you return to the first section and play it once, ending on the note indicated by *Fine*. The *D.S. al Fine* is an abbreviation derived from Italian. *D.S.* is short for *Dal Segno* ("from" the sign 𝄋") and *al Fine* means "to the end."

Son de Pedro Pineda

Tr. 95

Mexican folk song
from Tierra Caliente
arr. J. Reynoso

What To Do:
Note that many of the phrases in the tune above start on the "up beats" (see Lesson 17). For example, in the first measure of the first ending, the phrase starts on the "and" of the 2nd beat. Listen to the CD to get the rhythmic feel. You can also listen to the version by Mexican fiddler, Juan Reynoso.

 Tr. 96

March

C.P.E. Bach

6

11

cresc.

16

21

What To Do:

This piece includes many of the techniques we will explore in the next book including advanced dynamics, upper positions and an accompanying voice using rhythms different from the lead voice.

1) Note the "high" third finger in measure 6.

2) The sideways "hairpin" like symbols means to play gradually louder (<) or softer (>). The Italian word for "gradually louder" is *crescendo* and it is used in measure 15 to denote a gradual increase in volume until the last beat of measure 18.

3) The last note in the piece is written as the note G, played an octave above the G on the D string. To play this high G, you will need to shift your left hand into third position. This is an advanced technique you will learn more about in Book 2. For now, you can simply hop your third finger to the D string.

Tr. 97

Slide Finger Blues

(in C major)

M. Norgaard

What To Do:
This version in C major gives you an opportunity to practice sliding your first finger between low and regular position.

Tr. 98

Give Me Your Hand

Irish Air

What To Do:
This pretty Irish Air should be played with a smooth legato stroke. Many traditional recordings exist of this tune. You will hear that traditional Irish fiddlers often play the eighth notes unevenly at different points in the tune, and use ornamentation, such as grace notes and advanced melodic techniques.

Thoughts on Practice

Deciding to practice on a regular basis is one decision, and deciding what and how to practice is another. It is generally a good idea to "warm up" at the beginning of each practice session by focusing on fundamental posture and physical comfort with the instrument. You can do this by playing scales or open strings. The most important thing to think about is correct technique. Eventually the way you hold your instrument will become automatic. This will take a considerable amount of time. Even very experienced players pay very close attention to posture. To practice on an artist's level, you must pay attention to detail: the way each finger rests on the bow, the imprints on your left hand fingers, the height of your right elbow and of course, your intonation. The page you are on in the book, or what piece you can play, is not as important as HOW YOU PLAY! No one wants to hear a difficult piece of music played badly. The best way to develop your skill as a violist is to consistently play the pieces you know every day. Your technical and musical growth should be evident by the way you play very simple things, very beautifully.

Practice Checklist

Check your instrument posture	Check your bow hold	Check your left hand
• Is the instrument supported by the shoulder rest? • Are your shoulders relaxed? • Is your head centered over your spine and not hanging forward?	• Are all joints curved? • Is your thumb bent and not protruding through the frog? • Are fingers relaxed? • Is your pinky sitting on top of the stick?	• Are fingers curved over the fingerboard? • Is your hand relaxed and free to move around the fingerboard? • Is your wrist straight?

Suggested Review Schedule

When you are working in Lessons 1-12, you should practice all the exercises and pieces you have learned everyday. From Lesson 13 until you complete the book, play your two most recent pieces daily and use the review rotation chart below on alternating practice days to insure comprehensive review of all learned material.

When you are working in Lessons 13-18 alternate between the two review lists below.

Technique Review from Lessons 1-5	Technique Review from Lessons 6-12
Sail Away Ladies	Sing-a-Ling-a-Ling
Old MacDonald Had a Farm	French Folk Song
Wildwood Flower	Bile Them Cabbages Down
Technique Review from Lessons 13-15	Technique Review from Lessons 16-18
Ach Du Lieber Augustine	Armenian Lullaby
Paddy Whack	Awesome Octaves

When you are working in Lessons 19-25 alternate between the four review lists below.

Technique Review Lessons 1-5	Ach Du Lieber Augustine	Bile Them Cabbages Down	Any 5 Technique Exercises
Sail Away Ladies	Paddy Whack	Technique Review, 19-25	Theme from Beethoven
Old MacDonald Had a Farm	Technique Review, 6-12	Armenian Lullaby	The Rakes of Mallow
Wildwood Flower	Sing-a-Ling-a-Ling	Awesome Octaves	Give Me Your Hand
Technique Review, 13-18	French Folk Song	Danish Folk Tune	Old Joe Clark
Planets Aligned	Marry The Piper Girl	Yankee Doodle	Marsk Stig's Daughters
In The Bleak Midwinter	St. Anthony's Chorale	Rigadoun	First Western Change
Blackberry Blossom	The Bridge of Avignon	Scotland the Brave	March
Gavotte	Slide Finger Blues (in C major)	Son de Pedro Pineda	Slide Finger Blues (in D)

Index of Terms

Answer Key

Pg. 12: 1) quarter; 2) whole; 3) half; 4) whole; 5) quarter; 6) half; 7) quarter; 8) half; 9) whole; 10) half.
Pg. 16: 1) ascending; 2) ascending; 3) descending; 4) ascending.
Pg. 24: G, A, C, D, C, A, G, D.
Pg. 24: G, A, D, B, A, E, D, A, G, C, D, D, A, G.
Pg. 41: Kookaburra (key of D), Harvest Song (key of G), Sing-a-Ling-a-Ling (key of G), Wildwood Flower (key of G), Armenian Lullaby (key of E minor, you'll learn about minor in Book 2), Danish Folk Song (key of A minor) and St. Anthony's Chorale (key of G).
Pg. 48: 1) Duple; 2) triple; 3) triple; 4) triple; 5) duple; 6) triple; 7) duple; 8) duple.
Pg. 53: 1) Octave; 2) no; 3) no; 4) octave; 5) octave; 6) no; 7) no; 8) octave.
Pg. 56: 1) Fifth; 2) octave; 3) octave; 4) fifth; 5) octave; 6) octave; 7) fifth.
Pg. 63:

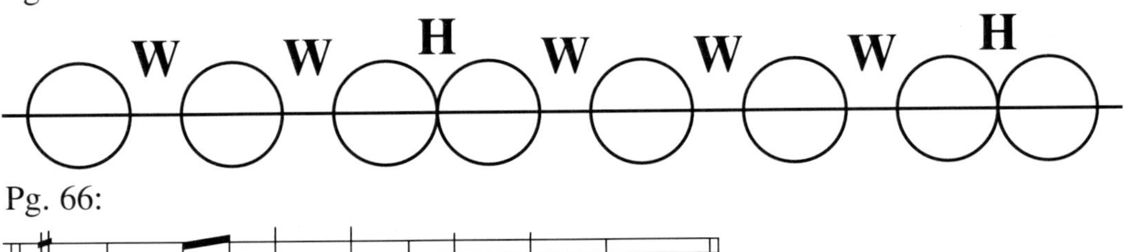

Pg. 66:

Pg. 69: G up to A: step; F up to E: skip; G up to D: skip; C down to F: skip; C up to D: step; B down to A: step
Pg. 69: 3rd up; 5th up; unison; octave down; 6th up; 2nd down; 4th up; 9th down.
Pg. 75: F♯/2 high; F/2 low; D/open; F/2 low; F♯/2 high; G♯/3 high; A/open; B/ 1.

Viola Sizes

Violas come in different sizes. Whether you buy or rent a viola, it is very important to play on an instrument that is the correct size for you. Many different sized instruments are available to accommodate children's continuing growth. Sometimes, when small violas are not available, 1/2 or 3/4 sized violins can be restrung to viola tuning. This is not a recommended solution. The ribs of a viola are wider than the ribs of a violin, and the added resonating space is needed to allow the C string to vibrate freely. When a small child needs a viola smaller than 11" however, this may be the only solution.

Violas come in the following sizes; 11", 12", 13", 14, 14 1/2", 15", 15 1/2", 16", 16 1/2", and 17". A 14" viola, which is the same size as a full-sized violin, is considered to be a 3/4 size viola. Although it is possible for smaller violas to produce a rich full sound, most adults and high school-aged students play a 16" viola. Middle school students usually play a 13" or 14" viola and elementary-aged students usually play an 11" or 12" viola.

There are a few good ways to help you determine what size instrument you should use. Generally, you should be able to place the instrument on your left shoulder, place your head on the chinrest and extend your left hand underneath the viola the length of the instrument, and wrap your fingers around the scroll.

Another way to assess size is to have someone compare the length of the body of the instrument to the width of your back from shoulder to shoulder. The body of the viola should not be longer than the width of your shoulders. Do not let anyone talk you into playing an instrument that is the wrong size. It is much better to play on a smaller, rather than larger instrument.

A large instrument is not something you "grow into" while you are learning to play. In many ways it's like buying a perfectly sized pair of shoes. The right fit is extremely important.

Chinrests and Shoulder Rests

One goal of basic viola posture is to position the instrument on the shoulder without tension in the head, neck or shoulders. Obviously you will know you have a viola on your shoulder, but you should be able to be relaxed and without discomfort when the viola is in the correct playing position.

Chinrests

The term "chinrest" is somewhat a misnomer. In actuality, chinrests are designed to accommodate your jawbone and to aid in supporting the viola. Most chinrests are concave (saucer shaped) designed so you can "hook" your jawbone over the edge. If you initially feel uncomfortable when placing the viola under your jawbone, check to be sure you are not resting your jawbone ON the edge of the chinrest. Chinrests come in different shapes and sizes. While most chinrests are attached to the instrument next to the tailpiece, there are chinrests designed to be centered on the instrument resting over the tailpiece. Additionally, the placement of the chinrest may have to be adjusted. If your head consistently rests on top of the tailpiece, you may want to try an over-the-tailpiece chinrest. Local suppliers can be helpful in allowing you to try different chinrests and shoulder rests in the store.

Shoulder Rests

Feeling comfortable while playing the viola should certainly be one of your first goals. You should be able to consistently place your instrument in a comfortable position that allows total freedom of the left arm, with shoulders, head, and neck muscles relaxed. All violists should use some sort of shoulder rest. Shoulder rests are designed to fill the space between the viola and your shoulder. They help support the viola and keep the instrument stable while you are playing. Shoulder rests are designed to prevent unnecessary tension and injury, allowing you to relax without raising your shoulder to hold the viola.

Many professional styles of shoulder rests exist and you should continue to try different brands and styles until you really feel comfortable. Most standard shoulder rests have adjustable parts that allow you to somewhat customize the height and angle of the rest. Shoulder rests are placed on the back of the instrument, and attached in a variety of ways. Some players prefer to use an egg-crate sponge cut to size or a small pad instead of a commercial shoulder rest.

You may be very comfortable using the chinrest and shoulder rest that are on your viola. If you are not however, take the time to try other styles of chinrests and shoulder rests until you find just the right fit. If you have a local music dealer, they may allow you to try different styles in the store or to take a few home on a trial basis until you find one that is comfortable. In any case you need to have one!!

Putting on the Shoulder Rest

Shoulder rests should be attached to the viola at the bottom on the back of the instrument. Sponges can be attached by using a rubber band around the viola or by hooking the rubber band around the corner of a bout and the end button. Most commercial shoulder rests can only be attached to the viola in one way. Use logic, and fill in the space between the viola and your chest with the highest section of the shoulder rest.

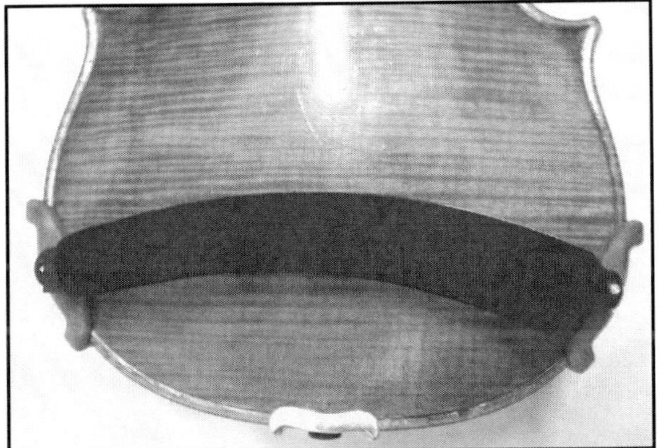

Shoulder rests and chinrests are indispensable accessories.

Opening the Case for the First Time

When you open your viola case for the first time, take a few minutes to check the basic condition of the viola. Make sure your viola is adjusted properly and the strings and other parts of the instrument itself are in good playing condition. This will help make your first experience with the instrument more successful. A viola CAN sound great, right from the beginning. Good strings and a well-adjusted instrument will help.

- Make sure the bridge is perpendicular to the instrument. Bridges warp over time and may need to be replaced. If the bridge is leaning slightly, you can straighten it out by holding the instrument with the end button braced on your lap, two thumbs on one side of the bridge and forefingers on the other side of the bridge. Very carefully "coax" the bridge until it is straight. If the bridge is too warped to stand straight with very little encouragement, it will have to be replaced.

- Look inside the instrument to be sure the sound post is standing up straight. If the sound post is crooked or is rolling around inside the instrument, you will need to have it professionally repaired. This is usually an easy and inexpensive adjustment.

- Check to be sure the strings are not frayed or broken. If you need to change the strings, change one string at a time, threading the string in the peg left open by the removed string. Never take all the strings off the instrument at the same time. This will take too much tension off the top of the viola, and the sound post (which is only held in place by the tension created between the top and bottom of the viola) will fall.

- Always have an extra set of strings in your case. Strings last for varying amounts of time depending on a multitude of factors. Obviously if you break a string, you need to change it. Strings should also be changed when they fray or go "false." You will know when a string is false when you have difficulty tuning the string or when you hear the string change pitch when you play with heavy bow weight.

- With some instruction and common sense you can perform the following basic maintenance on your instrument yourself: changing strings and replacing fine tuners.

- While you can perform basic maintenance on the viola yourself, you should not attempt to make major repairs on the viola or the bow. The following situations require professional intervention:

  - cracks in the instrument
  - warping of the fingerboard
  - bow rehairing
  - warped or broken bridge
  - open seams
  - collapsed sound post
  - broken tailpiece or pegs

- The following are a few of the accessories that you will want to keep in your case at all times:

  - cleaning cloth
  - rosin
  - extra strings
  - shoulder rest
  - pencil
  - nail clippers

- As a violist, you will need to keep your hands clean and your fingernails clipped. It is not possible to achieve a correct hand position on the viola with long fingernails. The pads of the fingers on both hands play an integral role in achieving good tone and bow control.

It is important to keep the viola from being exposed to intense heat or cold. Never leave your viola in a hot car or directly next to a heater or air conditioner. The viola can crack, seams can open, varnish can become damaged and it will most likely go out of tune. You will get used to taking your viola with you, like you would your child, protecting it from being too hot, too cold, or from being stolen!

Placing Fingerboard Tapes

In the beginning stages of learning to play the viola, you will probably want to use fingerboard markers on your viola to help you know where to put your fingers. There are many ways to mark the fingerboard, including commercially sold tapes that create a fingerboard grid, almost like frets on a guitar. We suggest using colored tape to indicate placement for the first finger (the note B on the A string), high second finger (C♯ on the A string), third finger (D on the A string) and fourth finger (E on the A string).

Using a special kind of tape is not necessary, however choose tape that is thin or can be cut thin. Some people use auto striping tape because it is already cut very thin and can be placed very precisely. Reference the diagram below to help you place tapes on your fingerboard. Use an electronic tuner or piano to match placement of the tapes to the indicated notes.

Using fingerboard markers is somewhat controversial. Some teachers feel that marking the fingerboard keeps students from developing a sense of pitch on their own. Our goal in using fingerboard markers or tapes is to allow repeated correct placement of the fingers, resulting in repeated, correct pitches. When kinesthetic memory is developed and the ear has experienced the sound of correct intonation, students will become less dependent on the tapes and may start removing them one at a time. There are innumerable endeavors in life that enlist aids in developing kinesthetic memory. In a way you are "tracing" the fingerboard grid. When the tapes are gone, you should continue to think of the fingerboard as a grid of interrelated pitches.

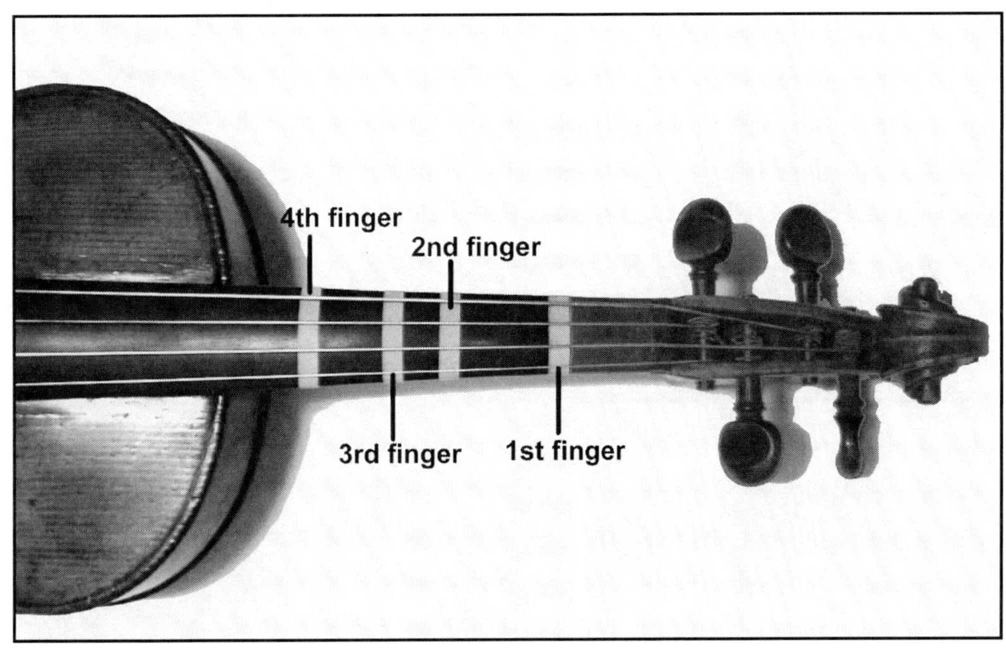

Preparing the Instrument to Play

Each time you prepare to play, you will need to tighten and rosin the bow, put on the shoulder rest, and tune the instrument.

- Tighten the bow just enough to create resistance between the bow stick and the hair. When you put weight on the bow, you want the bow to feel strong so you can produce a big tone. Never over-tighten the bow, and remember to loosen the hair of the bow before putting the bow in the case.
- You should put rosin on the bow hair to create traction for the bow as you pull it across the strings. Rosin is made from tree sap. There are many different brands of rosin available. Once you choose a brand of rosin, it works well to keep using that brand until the next time you re-hair the bow. Usually 5 - 10 swipes of rosin per practice is sufficient. Applying too much rosin can make the tone scratchy and leave rosin dust everywhere.
- Wipe off the instrument and strings after each playing session. The rosin dust can build up, and actually damage the varnish on the instrument.

Never touch the hair of the bow. The oil and dirt from your hands can keep rosin from sticking.

- Put the shoulder rest or sponge on the back of the viola. (see pg. 83)

Tuning the Viola

Track 1 (Tuning note A), Track 2 (D), Track 3 (G), Track 4 (C)

Your viola strings are tuned in intervals of "fifths," five notes or musical alphabet names apart (Lesson 1). The strings of the viola are tuned to the notes C, G, D, and A. The first four tracks of the CD include these pitches in the following order: Track 1, Open A string; Track 2, Open D string; Track 3, Open G string; and Track 4, open C string.

The viola is tuned by using pegs and fine tuners. Turning the pegs or fine tuners clockwise will tighten the string and raise the pitch; counterclockwise will loosen the string and lower the pitch. If the viola is only slightly out of tune, use the fine tuners. Most violas will come with a fine tuner on the A string. This is because the A string is the thinnest and most delicate string and can break easily from too much tension. For beginning students we suggest putting fine tuners on all four strings. It makes tuning easier and may save you from breaking strings while you are learning to tune the instrument.

Beginning students often break strings by over-tightening the string, turning the peg or fine tuner too far or too fast. Use caution and patience when tuning!!

To tune the viola, use the CD as a pitch reference. You can also use a tuning fork, metronome with tuning pitches, an electronic tuner, or a four-note pitch pipe. Electronic tuners are probably your best choice. The goal is to match the tuning of your strings to the pitch referent. In the beginning stages of tuning you will be tuning by plucking the strings. Later you will learn to tune using the bow (see below). Do not bring just one string fully up to pitch if the viola is very out of tune and the strings are all very loose. Bring ALL the strings closer to pitch gradually. Tuning one string when the others are very loose will cause uneven tension on the bridge. If the bridge does fall, the sound post may fall also, and then you will need to take the instrument for repair.

Because the pegs are conical, you need to turn and push to keep them in place. When tuning, hold the viola facing you with the tail button resting in your lap (see picture). You will use both hands for tuning. One hand will hold the instrument and create an opposing force for the other hand, which will either turn the pegs or stabilize the instrument if you are using the fine tuners.

Start by using the pitch A (Track 1) as the referent note. With your left hand on the upper bout of the viola, pluck the A string with your left thumb and turn the A peg with your right hand (see picture). Listen for a match in pitch. If the pitch of the string matches the tuning note, GREAT!!! If not, you need to decide if the pitch of the string is too low or too high. If it is slightly out of tune, use the fine tuners. Otherwise, use the pegs. If you use the pegs, slightly loosen the string (counter clockwise turn) then push in and turn the peg clockwise while you are plucking the string until you reach the pitch. Next, tune the D string (Track 2). When tuning the G (Track 3) and C strings (Track 4), the right hand holds the bout and plucks the string, and the left hand turns the pegs or fine tuners.

Once you learn to hold the bow and the viola, you should tune while bowing (see picture).

Some tuners, and of course the piano, provide a referent pitch for each string. Other tuners and metronomes only produce the note A. If you use a piano or tuner with pitches, repeat this process with each string. Don't be discouraged if you are having difficulty tuning. A teacher or experienced player can provide much insight into the tuning process.

Learning to tune independently is a long process. Don't hesitate to ask for help.

About the Authors

Martin Norgaard is the author of the groundbreaking methods *Modern Violin Method, Modern Viola Method, Getting Into Gypsy Jazz Violin, Jazz Fiddle Wizard, Jazz Fiddle Wizard Junior, Jazz Viola Wizard Junior,* and *Jazz Cello Wizard Junior Volumes 1* and 2 for Mel Bay Publications. In addition, Norgaard is the composer of several string orchestra pieces for FJH Music Company. He completed his doctoral studies in Music and Human Learning at The University of Texas at Austin.

Norgaard taught jazz and commercial strings at Belmont University and Vanderbilt University in Nashville for six years, and was director of the Belmont Jazz String Quartet and Jazz String Septet, which were featured at IAJE 2001, MENC 2002 and ASTA 2003.

Norgaard is a frequent clinician at state, national and international conventions such as Singapore International String Conference, ASTA, TMEA, SAA, OMEA, IMEA, GMEA, MENC, and IAJE, and has taught at summer workshops such as the IAJE Teacher Training Institute, the South Carolina Suzuki Institute, the Santa Fe Suzuki Institute, the Augusta Heritage Festival and Vanderbilt's International Fiddle School. Check out his web site at JazzFiddleWizard.com.

Laurie Scott is Assistant Professor of Music and Human Learning at The University of Texas at Austin. Additionally, she serves as the director of The University of Texas String Project. Previous to this appointment, Dr. Scott served as professor of violin and viola and director of music education studies at Southwestern University in Georgetown, Texas. She holds a master's degree in applied violin from the University of Nebraska, and a bachelor's degree in music education from the State University of New York at Fredonia. She received her Ph.D. in Music Education from the University of Texas. Most recently she received both The University of Texas School of Fine Arts Teaching Excellence Award and the School of Music Teaching Award. She is a guest clinician and conductor at state and national conventions speaking on string pedagogy, public school music education, and character development through the arts. Her articles have appeared in *The American String Teacher, The American Suzuki Journal,* and *The Journal of Research in Music Education.* In May of 2006, the Suzuki Association of the Americas designated Dr. Scott as a teacher trainer for *Suzuki in Schools.*

Many of the ideas presented in this book are further developed in the following books Scott co-authored with William Dick: *Mastery For Strings: A Longitudinal Sequence of Instruction for School Orchestras, Studio Lessons, and College Methods Courses* and *Mastery for Strings: Navigating the Fingerboard* (for more information, visit *masteryforstrings.com*). These books specifically address the teaching of technique in heterogeneous string class settings.

Audio Credits

Curtis Jones – Guitar
Holly Jones – Vocals
Melissa Beeker – Viola
Martin Norgaard – Violin, Piano
Laurie Scott – Viola, Violin

Dan Dickey – Vihuela, Guitarrón
Graeme Francis – Percussion
John Gordon – Bass
Wade Harper – Bagpipes

Jazz Rhythm Section:
Jim White – Drums
Charlie Chadwick – Bass
Bruce Dudley – Piano